Balletmaster

Balletmaster

A Dancer's View of George Balanchine

Moira Shearer

G. P. PUTNAM'S SONS
New York

For Г. М. БАЛАНЧИВАДЗЕ

G. P. Putnam's Sons
Publishers Since 1838
200 Madison Avenue
New York, NY 10016

Library of Congress Cataloging-in-Publication Data

Shearer, Moira, date.
Balletmaster: a dancer's view of George Balanchine.

Includes index.
1. Balanchine, George. 2. Choreographers—
United States—Biography. I. Title.
GV1785.B32S53 1987   792.8'2'0924 [B]   86-30601

ISBN 0-399-13184-1

Printed in the United States of America
1 2 3 4 5 6 7 8 9 10

Contents

Foreword

So often books and articles about the ballet are weighed down with technicalities and critical analysis which I feel can only be of interest to the student, the professional and the intense balletomane. This book is for the general reader.

George Balanchine was an exceptional, multi-talented man whose life was in some ways a strange one. Discovering its details has been fascinating for me and I hope may prove equally absorbing to people quite unconnected with the ballet.

To be a dancer or a choreographer is not a rarified occupation: it is a job of work like any other, though perhaps it requires more physical strength, stamina and discipline than many. Balanchine sometimes described himself as a carpenter, the creation of a ballet being not dissimilar to the construction of an intricate and beautiful piece of furniture. Such an attitude can soften public unease about the ballet, removing a mystique which is purely imaginary. In this book I have tried to do the same.

I have been given generous help by many people, some of whom I have known for years and others whom I have met for the first time. I am deeply grateful for the time and the information they have given me and which have made my visits to New York and London such a pleasure. In America I would like to thank Brigitta Lieberson; Maria Tallchief; Tamara Geva; Agnes de Mille; Robert Irving; Clive Barnes; Genevieve Oswald, curator of Dance at the Library of the Performing Arts, and also her team of most willing assistants; William Como, editor of Dance Magazine, and Lincoln Kirstein, the father of the School of American Ballet. My special thanks to a dear friend from the past, Alexandra Danilova – the first ballerina I ever saw, in *La Boutique Fantasque* at Covent Garden in 1934. And to Barbara Horgan, personal assistant and secretary to Balanchine for many years. She is a new friend who has shown me remarkable kindness, checking the American section of my manuscript for inaccuracies and giving much help and encouragement.

In London I would like to thank Ninette de Valois; Alicia Markova; Frederick Ashton; and another dear friend of many shared memories and experiences, Beryl Grey.

Susan Hill of Sidgwick and Jackson and her invaluable assistant, Rowena Webb, and Alan Williams of Putnam's in New York have been tolerant, patient and immensely helpful and I am also indebted to Vickie Cousins, a wizard of the word processor, who typed the final manuscript.

For permission to quote from published material my grateful thanks to Bernard Taper and Random House (*Balanchine – a Biography*): to Solomon Volkov and Simon and Schuster (*Balanchine's Tchaikovsky*): and to John Gruen and Viking (*The Private World of Ballet*). Anne-Marie Ehrlich in London and Jane Emerson of Ballet Society in New York have toiled over the collection of photographs for which I am most grateful.

Lastly, my family. My husband, who has been a professional writer for more than forty years, has been my most tough and uncompromising critic – sometimes causing me deep depression and suppressed fury but teaching me many invaluable things about writing. I cannot thank him adequately. And my children, all now busy with their own lives, have given me wonderful encouragement with their unfailing interest – and amusement too, at the sound of *two* typewriters now clacking in our house.

Moira Shearer
Wiltshire

Prologue

It was early spring 1950 and I had been married for three weeks. A call was posted up on our notice board at the Royal Opera House, Covent Garden for a first full company rehearsal with George Balanchine. He had come from New York to produce his *Ballet Imperial*, which he had originally choreographed for Ballet Caravan in 1941. We were all there that morning when he walked on to the stage escorted and introduced by our director, Ninette de Valois. A beautiful man, I thought – elegant, dapper, wearing a light grey suit, polished shoes and a tiny flower in his buttonhole, with, above it, a marvellous Mongolian face.

No one in the company had seen this *Ballet Imperial*. The music was Tchaikovsky's 2nd Piano Concerto, and our rehearsal pianist with her piano score was waiting at an old upright in the corner. Mr Balanchine went to work at once. Immediately I was struck by his calm, gentle manner: the quietness of his voice which nevertheless carried absolute authority. Gradually the first movement of the ballet took shape – he was working with the first cast of principals, Margot Fonteyn in the leading rôle. The second and third casts for this, myself and a charming Russian, Violetta Elvin, were in the background watching and listening.

The days passed and the ballet was completed. To me it was a fascinating experience, made even more so by two astonishing moments. The first came when the leading male dancer failed to perform a series of difficult turns in the air exactly as

Mr Balanchine wanted. Now, shedding his jacket, this much
older man, quite unprepared and in his polished shoes, showed
him how it should be done: beautifully – apparently effortlessly. Most people would have broken a bone. The second moment
was even more impressive. A passage in the extremely taxing
piano score was not quite as he wanted it. After some discussion with the pianist he asked her to move from the piano stool.
Taking her place, he played the entire section with the exact
variations of tempo that he required. I already knew that he was
the most musical of choreographers, but this mastery of the
piano was a revelation. I was hopelessly in love with him for a
full ten minutes.

All was ready for the first night. Mr Balanchine was still with
us, supervising final rehearsals and attending the opening
performance. I was scheduled to dance five days later, and
Violetta Elvin later still. At Covent Garden the formula for
second and third casts was always the same. There were no
rehearsal rooms in the theatre in the 1940s and 1950s so,
supervised by a ballet master, we were given two or three
runs-through with our partners in a basement in Kingsway or in
an army drill hall in Chenies Street. Then we were 'on' – first
time on the stage, first time in costume, first time with the
orchestra and full company. Our first performances were virtually dress rehearsals and the critics came to judge us sternly.
It was tough, but we were used to it.

Coming in one morning, I was stunned to read on the notice
board a rehearsal call for myself and John Hart with
Mr Balanchine. I have heard since that he had asked for this,
and a refusal to a distinguished guest would, I suppose, have
been difficult. I went to my dressing room and sat thinking for a
while. It was unprecedented: a private rehearsal with Balanchine, and on the stage, not in the coke-fumed basement or
dusty drill hall. Then I thought about the rôle. *Ballet Imperial* is
a ballet without a story, simply classic dancing in the grand
manner. But for the leading dancer there is one great difference.
I had watched Balanchine closely at all the rehearsals with the
first cast and had seen what he seemed to want: virtuoso
dancing as we all know it in *Sleeping Beauty* and *Swan Lake* –

and yet, not quite. There was an original twist to everything –
few movements were straight and severely perpendicular. They
were tilted, angled dangerously, and off-balance – literally; this
interested me very much. He hadn't pressed the point after the
first rehearsals and I wondered whether, when it came to my
own performance, I would be allowed to attempt this strange
acrobatic slant. Also I had no idea if I could do it.

It was time. We were on the stage in the dreary working light
waiting for him. I was very nervous. He arrived, elegant as
always. We had never really met, so we all shook hands and he
made some courteous small talk for a few minutes as if at a
cocktail party. Then, nodding to the pianist, he said, 'So – let us
begin.' He stood with his back to the dropped curtain and I
walked to an upstage corner for the first entrance.

This is the piano cadenza in the first movement of the
concerto: technical fireworks from the pianist, similarly from
the dancer. Indeed this rôle mirrors the solo instrument
throughout the ballet. Waiting for the first notes, I realized that I
hadn't the least notion whether I could do what I was about to
attempt, but I remember thinking, 'This is a marvellous chance.
You've nothing to lose – just have a go.'

The cadenza begins quietly and slowly. I saw his face briefly
– impassive, enigmatic. Then the tempo builds until one is a
whirling mass and there is no time to be aware of anything. The
pianist struck the final chord, which signalled the entry of the
orchestra, I disappeared into the wings, and there was dead
silence. It hadn't been good, I knew – I had missed so many
things that I had imagined in my mind's eye. I walked back on
to the stage in the usual dancer's state – glistening face, heaving
diaphragm – and waited. He came towards me with a charming,
surprised expression, put his hands round my face and kissed
me.

Looking back over thirty-seven years, I realize that the next
few minutes of that day were the most important in my career as
a dancer. This man, whom I hardly knew, gave me something
invaluable, something I lacked totally – self-confidence. Until
that day this lack of confidence and my consequent vulnerability was almost a joke. I could be mashed into the ground so
easily – and frequently was, vulnerability in others being such

good sport. Did Mr Balanchine sense this? I shall never know. I only know that he gave genuine praise for my efforts, showed his interest and pleasure and, above all, showed me that he believed in me. It was extraordinary.

We worked on until the ballet was complete. One prodigious technical hurdle followed another, and if I seemed to falter he simply said, 'Go on – go on, I know you can do it.' I began to believe in myself, and found that I was performing everything that he wanted, the dangerous slanting way, even the nearly impossible. It was an exhilarating experience.

He gave me three further brief rehearsals; they were magical moments and I learned so much from this remarkable man – not only about how to dance but about myself. I believe I was a 'Balanchine dancer', though in 1950 this term had still to be invented. Had I not just been married and with my life about to take a new turn, I think I would have followed George Balanchine back across the Atlantic in the hope of joining his New York City Ballet. Instead we never met again.

My debt to him is infinite, and this book about his life is my tribute.

Part 1

1
St Petersburg

George Balanchine, throughout his long life, never seemed quite sure whether he was a Russian or a Georgian. To him the distinction was great: Russians and Russian culture were oriental, but Georgians were 'Mediterranean' people – 'like Italians'. His father's family was Georgian, and he had inherited the temperament and many of the characteristics of a Georgian; a certain arrogance and cruelty, together with charm and great sociability. It was as a Georgian that he thought of himself, but he did not know his own country. In 1962, when he was fifty-eight, he visited Georgia for the first time. He went first to Tbilisi, and then to his father's birthplace, Koutais, to find the house where his parents had lived after his departure from Russia in the 1920s.

Balanchine's dilemma came from his St Petersburg-born mother and his own birth and early childhood in that beautiful, Italianate city, so western in its thought and culture. After forty years in America, and near death, he could also say, 'I am from Petersburg – I am a Petersburger.' All his earliest memories and influences came from that city: the final, glittering tsarist years, the golden ceremonial displays of monarchy, church and state whose theatricality he had adored. As he came to the end of his life, these memories became more vivid than anything else.

Gyorgy Melitonovich Balanchivadze was born on 22 January 1904 to Meliton Balanchivadze, a composer, and his young second wife, Maria. Meliton, with two teenaged sons had been widowed some years before and had married again at the age of thirty-six. He was a happy, sociable, lusty man, immensely popular among his friends, most of whom were Georgians. He was a reasonably good composer: he had written an opera, *Tamara the Wily*, a Mass, many choral works and much church music. But it was as a collector and arranger of Caucasian folk music and song that he became known as the Georgian Glinka. This brought him a little fame but nothing more tangible. Luckily his delightful, convivial temperament was quite unperturbed by the family's lack of riches and they lived a happy, carefree life.

There were three children of this marriage, very close in age – Tamara, Gyorgy and Andrey. Maria, their mother, tiny, fair-haired and blue-eyed, came from a modest home but possessed great feeling and sensitivity for the arts. She loved music and was an excellent pianist, a talent she passed on to her elder son. Meliton may have been the noisy extrovert but it was the small, quiet mother who was the real influence and strength in their household. His close friend the ballerina Alexandra Danilova says that to the end of his life Balanchine always had '*la tendresse pour sa mère*'.

Before Gyorgy was two years old a strange and alarming event occurred. In 1905 his mother took him in his pram, with his sister, to one of the large St Petersburg parks. While the children played she noticed, sitting on a bench near them, an elegant, distinguished-looking man reading quietly in the sunshine. He was still there when they left for home. The next morning she read in the newspaper of the assassination of an important diplomat: a bomb had been thrown as he sat reading in a public park. The assassins, who had been caught, spoke of their vigil with the bomb – they had waited in order to avoid harming a young woman and her children who were playing nearby. Gyorgy, of course, could remember nothing of this, but an episode in the following year was very different. Again he was in a public place, this time at a fête in the open air where there were crowds of people round a raised stage. Now a toddler, he was suddenly separated from his mother. He was lost – crying and terrified – until a stranger picked him up, carried him on to the stage and held him up to be claimed.

Gyorgy remembered this frightening début upon a stage with real terror; it was his earliest memory.

Other childhood impressions were much happier, particularly St Petersburg Christmases. Though Easter was the great festival, with cathedral and church bells ringing through the night, Christmas appealed to Gyorgy even more. The city was very still, dark and mysterious, not at all like the frenetic celebrations in the west. He was taken to the Christmas service in St Vladimir's; there was a marvellous moment when all the candles were put out and, as everyone sat in darkness, the glorious sound of a Russian Orthodox choir was heard. He loved the processions – the priests, the deacons and altar boys in velvets and brocades – and was quite overcome by the climax of the service, the appearance of the glittering Metropolitan himself.

At home with his family, the tree was another source of wonder. He never forgot the scent of those St Petersburg Christmas trees, mixed with the waxy smell of many tiny burning candles. The decorations were gold paper angels and stars and beautiful large glass pears. Everything was covered in a veil of silver paper threads. One year he was given a watch which didn't work: wild excitement – not only to have a watch of his own, but one that wouldn't go. No other boy had that! Another year he opened a parcel to find an American toy car. Remembering it at the age of seventy-seven he told the writer Solomon Volkov, 'You wind it up and it goes – it was funny, strange and – nice!' During these years the Balanchivadzes went through a period of near-Chekhovian farce. Meliton bought a ticket in the state lottery; Maria checked the number and, convinced that he had the winning one, begged him to go to the state bank. He was too embarrassed, but finally she persuaded him. He had indeed won, 100,000 roubles (over £100,000) and he came home clutching his cheque.

Now the farce began. Generous, improvident man that he was, he gave every friend and every lame duck a handsome present. He opened Georgian restaurants in various parts of St Petersburg, but without the least idea how to run them profitably, and of course he was much too hospitable ever to ask any of his friends to pay their bills. The family moved into a large, twelve-room apartment and invested in a country house, the one sound investment that Meliton ever made. Maria wanted security for the children's futures: instead there were purchases like a splendid carriage and an equally splendid white horse to draw it. Meliton did not discover until too late that the horse was circus-trained. On hearing a band, it danced and pranced on its hind legs in a captivating fashion leaving a smashed carriage and bruised travellers in the gutter. The final reckoning came with his involvement in a factory producing foundry vats by a new process perfected in the west. Many crooks immediately battened on to Meliton, relieving him of what money he still possessed. He was declared a wilful bankrupt and sent to Kresty prison for two years. Maria preserved a marvellous fiction with the children: their father was away in the Caucasus gathering folksong material. Eventually he re-turned, walking up the path to their country house – jaunty, elegant, carrying a single red rose. They rushed to greet him, and family life was resumed in his happy-go-lucky way. It was many years before Gyorgy discoverd where that folksong gathering had taken Meliton.

The family now lived permanently in the country. Their house, the only tangible evidence of their fortune, was a two-hour journey to the north-west of St Petersburg near Lounatiokki in the province of Viipuri. Now part of Finland, in the early 1900s it still belonged to the vast Russian Empire. The Balanchivadzes lived in an attractive wooden house built in the rustic style of the time, and its greatest asset for young children was the setting, in apparently boundless woods of silver birch, pine and mountain ash. Nothing gives children more pleasure than freedom and an active physical life, and Gyorgy loved it. He showed an early aptitude as naturalist and gardener and worked hard in the vegetable garden, especially on the straw-berry bed. He loved the family mushroom-picking days, becom-ing an expert on all edible varieties. And, on his own, he searched the woods for the mountain ash berries which he would bring home for jam-making. This was an idyllic life for a young boy but one that would bring him his first tragedy.

He had a pet piglet who was devoted to his small master, following him everywhere, even on the furthest berry-gathering forays. Gyorgy adored that pig as only a child can. Then it happened – the pig grew and met the fate of a plump porker. The boy was so distraught and inconsolable after this loss that he became a rigid vegetarian for quite some time.

Luckily there were many other interests and occupations, in particular the beginning of his formal education. A tutor came to teach the children arithmetic, history, grammar and religion, and Gyorgy had already started piano lessons with his mother. These progressed so well that a large German woman was soon engaged to continue his studies. Like every young child faced with those black and white keys he loathed the perpetual practice, the scales and the boredom. But also, as for everyone of real talent, a magic day arrived when he suddenly understood what he was doing – how beautiful the sounds were, what music could mean. He never lost this understanding: it was one of the most important aspects of his life and the basis for everything he would do in the future. He was now six years old.

During this time Meliton remained a shadowy, distant figure, often touring with a choral group he had formed; he was rarely at home, and when he was he took little part in the boy's development. His mother was his guide in everything including his first visits to the theatre, albeit a very primitive one. In the woods near Lounatiokki stood a simple, wooden building where troupes of travelling players gave performances in the summer months. Maria took the children there regularly, but Gyorgy was unimpressed, indeed uninterested. The sight of actors upon a stage entertaining an audience meant nothing to him. Then one day, rambling in the woods by himself, he found the silent, deserted theatre and was drawn into the dressing rooms, under the stage, into the wings and on to the stage itself. As he looked out over the rows of empty seats, he felt something odd and strange: it wasn't exactly the road to Damascus, but it was something he never forgot. The theatre had cast its spell.

Something else cast its spell upon him when he was eight – feminine beauty. His first appreciation of it happened in – of all places – the dentist's chair. The Balanchivadzes attended the surgery of a pretty blonde dentist in her early twenties, whom Gyorgy thought very beautiful. Perhaps she left her mark on the impressionable boy: much later, with few exceptions, he would

always choose pretty blondes in their early twenties as companions or wives. He was a very susceptible fellow.

Of more immediate importance to him and to his mother was
a plan for his future. What would be his profession? In family
discussions with uncles, aunts and half-brothers two possibilities always seemed uppermost – a naval or military career, or
the church. His half-brother Apollon was a captain in the army,
and an uncle was a colonel; they admired Gyorgy's straight
back and his bearing and were convinced he was a born officer.
'Think how splendid he will look in uniform!' they said.
Gyorgy was not at all averse to the idea. But another uncle was
Bishop of Gori in Georgia, and the glamour of his position, his
robes and the ceremonies he conducted against a background of
heady, sonorous music – perhaps music composed by his own
father – was even more attractive to the boy. In the Cathedral of
Our Lady of Kazan in St Petersburg he had seen yet another
uncle being ordained as a priest: the ceremony of the secular
man being buried and his resurrection as a man of God. This
cathedral had a famous choir of two hundred boys' voices of
such beauty that their singing brought tears to the eyes. Gyorgy
was so affected by church ritual that, when he wanted to dress
up and play-act, he always chose to be a bishop, building an
altar of chairs and conducting the most theatrical of services. In
spite of this, however, the family decided that the navy should
be his career and he seems to have been happy and satisfied
with the choice.

So, at nine years old and with his sister Tamara, now ten and
a half, they caught the train to St Petersburg with Maria. First
they would go to the Naval Academy, where with luck Gyorgy
might be accepted as a cadet; then to the Imperial Theatre
School, where Maria hoped that Tamara might enter the ballet
school. Sitting in their compartment, both children were
excited and nervous.

2
Imperial School

That day in St Petersburg in 1913 was strange and memorable for Gyorgy. He had an early disappointment at the Naval Academy, where Maria was told that there were no places left for new cadets and so a full year would have to pass before Gyorgy could try again. On arrival at the Imperial School in Theatre Street they joined the queue of mothers and children seated on benches in a long corridor waiting for the auditions. One hundred and fifty girls and fifty boys for approximately twenty places – it didn't seem very hopeful, especially as Maria had no *protektsia*, no sponsor, for Tamara. To have your child's entrance examination sponsored by someone of importance and authority in the city was a great advantage.

Theatre Street was a cul-de-sac. The school, a long, beautiful building like a baroque palace, ran the full length of one side. Opposite was the Ministry of Culture, another baroque building where the Lord Chamberlain had his official apartments. At the top of the street, dominating both, was the Alexandrinsky Theatre for classic drama. To a child's eye it looked grand and overpowering.

While they waited, an official of the school whom Maria knew slightly stopped to talk. She told him about the problem of Gyorgy and his immediate education; he looked at the boy and suggested that, since he was in the line with his sister, he too might try for a place in the ballet school. Should he be chosen for the probationary year and dislike it, or prove untalented, there would be no harm done, and he would be there in St Petersburg for a second attempt at the Naval Academy. It seemed a reasonable idea, and Maria was grateful.

Auditions for young children at the Imperial School did not involve any dancing. The judges were looking for carriage and deportment, style of movement, good physical proportions and flexible limbs. Talent, or the lack of it, could show itself later. Interestingly, my own teacher, Nicholas Legat, had been a young jury member some years earlier when a nine-year-old boy was examined. The other jurors wanted to reject him, considering him ugly, badly shaped and without any natural grace or style. Legat, however, found him unusual and striking and persuaded the others to accept him. His name was Vaslav Nijinsky.

On entering the examination room, Gyorgy was made to walk up and down, to turn this way and that, to have his back flexed and his arms, legs and feet wiggled in various directions. It was an odd situation for a boy who, a few hours earlier, had expected to join the navy. The jurors must have liked what they saw, because later that day he was accepted into the ballet school while Tamara, ironically, was rejected.

Now something happened which is astonishing and, to me, incomprehensible. Maria and Tamara left for the station, caught the evening train and within two hours were back in the cosy house at Lounatiokki. Gyorgy was left without warning in the Imperial School: he knew no one, he had never seen a ballet and did not know what it was, he had no idea what he would be expected to do and was without any small toy or possession from home which could have helped him through his first hours of 'abandonment'. It was a nightmare for a sensitive child, and his immediate reaction was to run away.

He had an Aunt Nadia who lived in St Petersburg, and late in the evening, when it was already dark, she opened the door of her apartment to find him standing there. Hiding her amazement she took him in, warmed him by the fire and gave him supper while listening to his troubles. But she was adamant: whatever his reception might be, he must go back. Discipline at the school was strict, and she knew of children being expelled for behaviour of this kind. She took him back that night – the authorities were understanding, even kind, and Gyorgy was neither expelled nor punished.

This experience, like the terror of being lost as a two-year-old, had its effect on him. He developed a sense of detachment and self-sufficiency at a precociously early age. He also developed a nervous habit – little sniffs between words, which twitched his top lip and showed his two front teeth: the other boys in his year nicknamed him 'Rat'. Gyorgy was unpopular and had no particular friend in any class. His probationary year was a wretched and lonely one.

Never academically brilliant, he excelled in the only two subjects he enjoyed – music and religion. As for the ballet classes, he hated them. There seemed to be no point to the exercises and movements he was forced to do: they were both painful and, to his eyes, silly. Legs which naturally faced forwards had to be turned painfully outwards to face to the side: girls, with the same shape of feet as everyone else, had to dance on the points of their toes. At the age of nine Gyorgy found these things ridiculous. Someone who later shared these feelings is the British dancer-director William Chappell who, years ago in a ballet class of frenzied activity, was seen leaning languidly on the barre. When yelled at by the irate teacher to 'Go on and *do it!*' he drawled, not moving a muscle, 'Shan't – it's against nature.'

He was right: the technique of the ballet is indeed against nature, and the only justification for the pain endured is the finished result. But one must know what this is; one must be given the chance to see the apparent ease, effortlessness and beauty of classical dancing when performed by masters. In the west most pupils have seen performances by good professional companies before entering a ballet school; they have some idea of their goal. Gyorgy had none. It seems an amazing omission but, in the probationary year at the Imperial School, no student was given any opportunity to see a performance at the nearby Maryinsky Theatre. It is hard to understand when there were such exceptional dancers in the company, such a surge in choreographic ideas and – as it happened – such new art in all forms emerging in Russia at this time.

By the turn of the century the early rumblings of the turmoil that would soon engulf Russia were already evident socially, politically and artistically. The old tsarist order and the new liberalism overlapped in strange ways. One of the strangest was the tragi-comic experiment made by Count Leo Tolstoy, already during his lifetime the most revered of Russian writers. Some years before their emancipation he freed the serfs on his huge estates at Yasnaya Polyana, dressed himself as a peasant and spent the rest of his life attempting to live and work like a peasant from the comfort of his great house.

In the early 1900s two men of artistic genius were becoming known – Sergey Diaghilev, born in 1872, and Igor Stravinsky, born in 1882. Both were true Russians, loving their country's history, traditions and culture, and both had radically modern ideas for the future of this culture. Tchaikovsky, the greatest of the 'old' composers and worshipped by both men, had worked on in his traditional, romantic style until his death by suicide in 1893. Marius Petipa, originally from Marseilles, the creator and choreographer of the formally classic Tchaikovsky ballets, died in St Petersburg in 1907, only ten years before the Revolution.

In 1904, the year of Gyorgy's birth, there were two instances of the old versus the new culture and two particular reactions to the dilemma. Anton Chekhov's play *The Cherry Orchard* was produced for the first time at the Moscow Arts Theatre. Konstantin Stanislavsky, the celebrated actor, writer and director of this theatre, with many Chekhov triumphs behind him, behaved in a sadly conventional and unimaginative manner. Given a wonderful, subtle play about the hopeless social and political gulf of the time, and a wonderful part – that of the peasant Loupakhin who buys the estate with the cherry orchard – he showed his subservience to the establishment. He refused the rôle of Loupakhin in favour of that of Gaev, brother of the well-born owner, Lyubov Ranevskaya.

Simultaneously, in St Petersburg, the American dancer Isadora Duncan startled everyone with her first Russian dance recitals. Not a woman to recognize any establishment, she leaped barefoot with abandon on to the stage of the Maryinsky, amusing and irritating many but firing a young dancer and choreographer called Mikhail Fokine with revolutionary theatrical ideas. She was the first dancer to use music usually reserved for the concert hall – Chopin, Schumann, Brahms. This was her greatest influence on Fokine, whose ballet *Chopiniana* – later known as *Les Sylphides* – was written soon afterwards, using a nocturne, prelude, mazurka, and waltzes originally composed for solo piano. Diaghilev was impressed, believing that here might be the modern choreographic talent he wanted for a company he planned to create. The Ballets Russes was born, giving its first celebrated Paris season in 1909. Isadora would have been furious had she realized her contribution to its creation. It was the reverse of her intention: her own dancing was always free, untechnical and deliberately anti-balletic. She never liked the ballet. Taken some years later to a performance by Anna Pavlova, she sat motionless throughout. Asked afterwards if she had enjoyed Madame Pavlova's dancing, she said, 'She bows well.'

When Gyorgy started his education at the Imperial School he had never heard of Diaghilev, Fokine or any of the Maryinsky dancers. This state of ignorance continued throughout his first year: all his energies were concentrated on trying to conquer the difficulties which he faced each day. His only pleasure and relaxation seem to have been music and the piano. Music was a compulsory subject, and every student was expected to master at least one instrument. Gyorgy gradually became a little less unpopular and made several tentative friendships through his particular talent for the piano.

Something which he did enjoy from his very first day was the handsome uniform – dark blue with silver lyres embroidered on the velvet collars and on the caps, which were similar to those worn by the naval cadets. It was truly a 'court' school: all the children were educated and trained for the theatre at the expense of the imperial treasury. They became little servants of the Tsar, felt proud and special in their unique uniforms, and were naturally very monarchist in their attitudes. Because the Tsar's family and the highest aristocratic families spoke French in preference to Russian, the Imperial School teachers addressed their students in the French style. The terms for the steps of the ballet are, and always will be, in French so this seemed not unnatural. Thus Gyorgy (affectionately known as Yura) became Georges at the age of nine. Balanchivadze remained unchanged but this, too, would be given a French slant many years later by Sergey Diaghilev. But they were completely cut off from their families, and Georges suffered greatly from homesickness. At weekends and short holidays, when St Petersburg boys could go home, he was often almost by himself in the school. Once or twice his Aunt Nadia took him by train to Lounatiokki for the day, and occasionally one or other of his tutors took him to their homes for a weekend. But many times he sat at the piano, alone in the large, silent building and still only nine years old.

The year ended. The progress of all the probationary students was reviewed, and further auditions were held; Maria brought Tamara for a second attempt at the ballet school, and this time the little girl was successful. Georges passed smoothly into his second year as a fully fledged student, and a contented Maria returned home knowing that both children were now safely installed in St Petersburg. In Tamara's case it was to be short-lived. She was placed in the year above Georges; Alexandra Danilova, affectionately known as Shura, was also in this year and she remembers Tamara as a noisy, rumbustious girl – a great tomboy. One episode remains vividly in her memory. Several girls were playing, having fun in one of the large classrooms, when suddenly Tamara hit Shura quite hard. Shura, a quiet well-behaved girl from a good military family, was shocked; she still speaks of the incident with some distaste today. Tamara's dancing may well have been in the same robust mould, for she failed to survive the probationary year and was returned to Lounatiokki and the family.

One morning there was great excitement in the second-year class – the children were to appear in *The Sleeping Beauty* at the Maryinsky Theatre. Normally the boys and girls worked separately, but now they came together for rehearsals and costume fittings. The anticipation before the first performance was almost unbearable. When the day came, carriages in the Tsar's colours with the double eagle, and two liveried coachmen on each box, drew up in front of the school. The children in their uniforms stepped in, six to each of ten coaches, and in this romantic fashion they arrived at the Maryinsky. 'It was like *Cinderella*,' said Balanchine years later.

That evening was a revelation to Georges. The theatre itself was beautiful – decorated in peacock blue, white and gold, colours very similar to those in Marie Antoinette's little theatre at Versailles. The stage was much larger than he had imagined, and the décors and costumes were both delicate and magnificent. But for a child the great marvels were the transformation scene and the various spectacular effects. He saw a ship sailing across a lake; a wall of flame; and cascading fountains and trees and climbing plants gradually covering the sleeping palace. When he saw Karsavina, Kschessinska and his own young teacher Andreyanov as the Prince, he suddenly realized what the ballet could be. Georges was won over. He danced that night in the Garland Waltz in Act I, and was a cupid on a carriage in Act III; for the remainder of the performance he stood in the wings, fascinated. As he watched the principals receive their applause after the final curtain, his one ambition was to become a dancer of equal elegance, style and technical brilliance.

3
Revolution

For the next three years Georges' life followed a regular pattern. He slept in a dormitory for thirty boys; the girls lived on the floor above. There were many large classrooms for both lessons and ballet classes, a rehearsal room, a small theatre for the school performances, a lovely little chapel and an infirmary. Though they started work early each day, they were well cared for. Their beds were made for them and their clothes and towels tidied by servants whom Balanchine described as 'all handsome men in uniform, buttoned from top to toe'. The food served to these hard-working, energetic children was very good. They ate bortsch and bitkis in its delicious sour cream sauce, apricot pies and occasionally rakhat-lukum and halvah, the sweetest of eastern sweetmeats. On Sunday evening there were beef patties and macaroni, Georges' favourite.

His principal teacher was the dashing, leading male dancer at the Maryinsky, Samuil Andreyanov. Then in his early thirties, he was an ideal ballet master, his effectiveness as a teacher being enhanced by his greatly admired performances and, in his classes, showed charm and understanding mixed with a certain aloofness which brought him even greater respect. Georges was influenced by him in many ways, and this trait of understanding coupled with detachment was very characteristic of his own adult life as teacher and ballet master. Another teacher whom he loved was Pavel Gerdt, Andreyanov's father-in-law. Gerdt had been a celebrated dancer in his day and now taught mime and the mysteries of character make-up. Georges responded with gusto to his teaching, showing flair and humour as a comedian and in character work; he loved transforming himself into doddering old men, and frequently appeared as an ancient – ridiculous or sinister – in school performances.

The Maryinsky dancers often came to rehearse in the school's rehearsal room. The students were not supposed to linger by the glass doors watching them but they inevitably did, each boy choosing his own favourite among the ballerinas, falling in love with her and dreaming ecstatically of partnering her. Georges, perhaps prophetically, loved two ballerinas – Tamara Karsavina and the beautiful Yelisaveta Gerdt, Andreyanov's wife. It is interesting that some critics of the time thought her dancing 'too cool' and that one described her as 'too vegetarian' – similar criticism to that levelled at many of Balanchine's New York City ballerinas. Perhaps his preference was formed at this early age.

Although he was not particularly interested in history or literature, certain books appealed instantly to Georges. He loved a series of children's stories, popular at the time, which described the adventures of the *murzilki* – tiny creatures who were everywhere, inside the smallest objects, seeing everything. Later he spoke of his sadness that children of other countries did not know of these fascinating little people. He also enjoyed *Stiopka-Rastriopka*, a translation of the German *Struwwelpeter*, and, best of all, *Max and Moritz* by Wilhelm Busch. These lively, naughty boys got into every kind of mischief; they were idolized by their young readers, and even in late middle age Stravinsky was still able to quote whole passages of their pranks. A little later Georges read with pleasure Jules Verne, Sir Arthur Conan Doyle, and the adventures of Nick Carter. These came out each week in serial form in brightly-coloured cardboard covers; the boys kept them circulating round the dormitory at night. Later still Georges came to Lermontov, Tolstoy and, above all, Pushkin. Petersburgers – Tchaikovsky, Stravinsky and Balanchine among them – adored Pushkin, not only for his genius but because he was a European Russian. Balanchine remembered his poetry as 'light, majestic

and balanced – like Petersburg, like Mozart's music'. But in
1914 he was still enslaved by Max and Moritz.

Georges was a fortunate boy to have been part of this tsarist
patronage, so soon to end. The Tsar, Nicholas II, was deeply
interested in the Maryinsky and in the school: he poured
money into the spectacular productions, attended many performances and received the dancers in the royal box. One of the
dancers frequently presented was Mathilde Kschessinska: a star
of the company, she had been the Tsar's mistress before his
marriage and was now protected by the Grand Duke Andrey,
whom she was to marry in Europe after the Revolution. Perhaps
there was a certain piquancy for her in these formal meetings.
She was an amazing woman: I met her in Paris in 1944 after the
Liberation, chic and still very grand, swathed in the jewellery
given to her by her royal patrons. Her dance studio was one of
three famous Maryinsky establishments in Paris during the
1930s and 1940s. Olga Preobrajenska and Lubov Egorova, both
celebrated ballerinas, had continued their rivalry with
Kschessinska as teachers, but the contrast between them was
marked: in 1944 Preobrajenska and Egorova were clearly exhausted and shabby after the war years – Kschessinska might
have stepped out of a diamond-studded bandbox.

Balanchine always remembered his own presentation to the
imperial family. It followed a performance of *The Little Hump-
backed Horse* which ended with a German march, specially
added to the ballet at the Tsar's request. Afterwards, the
students who had taken part changed into their uniforms and
went in pairs to be presented. The family were seated; he
thought the tall Tsarina and her four daughters very beautiful –
the Tsar rather small, with slightly bulging, light-coloured eyes.
Georges was amused by the way he rolled his r's. Each boy was
given a silver box containing delicious chocolates and a lovely
porcelain mug decorated with blue lyres and the imperial
monogram. Many of the boys were too overwhelmed to eat their
chocolates; Georges not only ate every one but managed to lose
both his mug and his silver box, to his eternal regret.

Between 1913 and 1917 there were many opportunities for
Georges to see the Maryinsky performances and to take an increasing part in them. He danced the mazurka in *Paquita*, a

part that had also been danced by the ten-year-old Nijinsky, in his first professional appearance some years before. With several other boys he performed a charming Spanish dance in Fokine's *La Jota Aragonese*. He attracted attention as the King of the Mice and later as the child Prince in Tchaikovsky's *Nutcracker*, and when he was not on stage himself he was a constant presence in the wings. Several dancers in the company noticed his 'merciless' gaze. Felia Doubrovska, then a recent graduate from the school, was heard to say, 'There's a little boy who doesn't miss a thing.'

Georges' first solo part, in 1915, was that of 'A Monkey' in the ballet *Pharaoh's Daughter*, a rôle which called for much acrobatic leaping about in treetops while the celebrated Kschessinska darted to and fro below, trying to shoot him with bow and arrows. He loved this part, performing it with zest and ingenuity and feeling honoured and important to be sharing the stage with the prima ballerina. But his name was not on the programme; it said simply, 'A Student'.

Outside, in the real world, terrible things were happening. The First World War was scything through the youth of western Europe, and the Russians, fighting on several fronts, suffered their first major defeat at Tannenberg in East Prussia in August 1914. Russia had mobilized thirteen million men; within three years two million had died and thousands had been taken prisoner. Splendid courageous fighters, they were defeated as much by tsarist incompetence and corruption as by their enemy in the field. The supply line to the army was staggeringly inefficient: by the spring of 1915 young men and boys were being sent to the front without rifles to face the fully trained, fully equipped German and Austrian armies. Later that summer the Tsar personally assumed supreme command of all the Russian forces. It was the death-knell for thousands. In his fascinating book *Holy Russia* Fitzroy Maclean describes Nicholas II as 'worthy, ineffectual and of limited intelligence', adding that he managed to be 'both vacillating and obstinate, a particularly unhappy combination under the circumstances prevailing in his country at that time'.

But to the people of the ballet, closed in their monastic world, this man was their generous patron and benefactor. They saw little beyond their safe, secure lives – only a few were aware of the tragedy mounting around them. The 'one sugarless day per week' decreed in the Imperial School, 'for our boys at the front', was the single sign that anything untoward was happening. To the end of his life Balanchine retained his strong childhood impression of his Tsar as an earthly god. He saw all royals and heads of state in this image and, though happy in his adopted country, America, he would have been happier still if the President of the United States could have been granted full royal status. It was a touchingly comic attitude for such a vigorous and independent man, but perhaps an inevitable one after his early experience of the Imperial School.

By late 1916 it was no longer a question of *if* there would be revolution, but *when*. Terrorism, or 'nihilism' as Turgenev called it, had been a strong force since the late nineteenth century. Tsar Alexander II was assassinated in 1881 and harsh repression followed, but terrorist plots continued and many were successful. For his involvement in one of them a young man, Alexander Ulyanov was executed in 1887. His seventeen-year-old brother Vladimir was deeply affected by this event; he changed his name and became Lenin.

After the formation in 1898 of the Social Democratic Labour Party – the first Marxist party – which split into the Menshevik and Bolshevik factions, Lenin became the Bolshevik leader living abroad in Europe until his return in April 1917. Meanwhile, a group calling themselves the Social Revolutionaries, formed in 1900, assassinated one Grand Duke, one Minister of Education and two Ministers of the Interior. The people's misery was increased by heavy taxation and the Tsar's refusal to establish a proper constitutional government. The climax came on 22 January 1905 – Georges' first birthday – when vast crowds of working people, peaceful and unarmed, marched behind a priest, Father Gapon, to the Winter Palace to petition the Tsar; the order to fire was given, the Cossacks charged and hundreds were massacred. During the strikes, riots and mutinies of the next twelve years it wasn't surprising that so many of those in power, such as the diplomat near Maria Balanchivadze and her children in the park, were killed by terrorist bombs. Belated tsarist palliatives like the changing of the name St

Petersburg to the more Russian Petrograd were ineffective and faintly ridiculous.

So it finally happened, almost bloodlessly, in early March 1917. The immediate cause was shortage of food – there had been virtually no bread at all for weeks. Demonstrations and major strikes were organized, when thousands of workers came out into the streets, stoning the police. The Cossacks were called out, but this time they did nothing. Two regiments of the Imperial Guard went over to the people, opening the arsenal and giving weapons to the mob. On 15 March, under strong military pressure, the Tsar was forced to abdicate and the Revolution was achieved.

The indifference of many aristocrats was extraordinary. On the very day of the outbreak of the Revolution the French Ambassador, Maurice Paléologue, gave a dinner party in his embassy. In his memoirs he wrote that the single topic of conversation which fired everyone and gave rise to heated discussion was the respective merits of the Maryinsky ballerinas – who was the finest: Pavlova, Karsavina or Kschessinska?

The near-anarchy which gripped Russia in the following eight months was largely ignored by the old nobility in Petrograd. Councils, known as soviets, had sprung up all over the country; the provisional government was composed mainly of Mensheviks and Social Revolutionaries, with the Bolsheviks forming a small minority. Lenin's secret return from Switzerland on 16 April was the signal for a major power struggle. The firebrand Trotsky formally joined the Bolsheviks in July: their attempt then to bring down the government failed but, though Lenin had to escape temporarily to Finland, the Bolsheviks gradually established complete ascendancy in the Petrograd Soviet. Lenin slipped back to the city in early October and made his way to the Bolshevik headquarters at Smolny, once a famous school for the daughters of the aristocracy.

On 7 November his moment came: garrison troops seized all the main buildings, and the cruiser *Aurora*, anchored in the River Neva with her guns trained on the government headquarters in the Winter Palace, fired salvoes of blanks as it too was taken. The Bolsheviks, though still a minority faction, were in power. It was all over quickly and remarkably quietly.

The life of the city seemed to go on much as usual: schools and offices were open and performances of opera and ballet were given to rapturously full houses. A friend of Alexander Kerensky, the Menshevik leader and now deposed head of government, walked that evening along the Neva and met an excited friend. 'Ah, my dear fellow,' he said, 'how sad that you missed it – he was in wonderful voice tonight.' Fyodor Chaliapin had given a memorable performance in *Don Carlos* at the Maryinsky. This little vignette could have been written by Chekhov; and if *The Cherry Orchard* had played that night at the Alexandrinsky, the dead writer would have laughed aloud.

The Ballet School, no longer Imperial, but continuing its traditional teaching during the revolutionary months, also fell to the Bolsheviks. Red sailors appeared in the corridors and dormitories searching for tsarist agents and sympathizers, and the school and company were closed down as 'decadent, counter-revolutionary institutions'. Georges and his friends were turned into the streets. He was now fourteen.

Meliton, Maria, Tamara and Andrey came to Petrograd, and for some months the whole family lived in an apartment on Bolshoi Moskovska beside Aunt Nadia. Life became increasingly hard: there was little food, a cold winter approached and money had become valueless. Meliton left for Tbilisi in the spring of 1918 – as a well-known artist and liberal, he became Minister of Culture in the new Republic of Georgia, but it was to be a short-lived post in a short-lived republic. He continued happily enough as the 'Georgian Glinka' and, after a difficult journey, Maria, Tamara and Andrey joined him there. Georges was left in Petrograd with Aunt Nadia, in case the school should reopen. Though he did not know it, this was to be the end of his family life. He never saw his mother, father or sister again.

For everyone living in Petrograd at this time life became a matter of survival. People took any kind of work they could find, not for money but for scraps of food – even potato peelings to make a watery soup. Soon there wasn't a single dog or cat to be seen: every pet, however loved, had been eaten. One morning Georges saw a dreadful sight: an old, sick horse dropped dead in the street, and within minutes men and women with knives rushed to it from every nearby house. A few more minutes and there was nothing left. He never forgot it.

Though still so young, he was a great help to his aunt. He worked as a messenger boy, then as a saddler's assistant stitching canvas girths. In the evenings he played the piano in a grubby little surburban cinema accompanying the silent comedies of the German Max Linder. His wages were crusts of bread, coffee grounds, and the ubiquitous potato peelings. During this period of civil war martial law was in force, and with street barricades and frequent sniper fire from windows and alleyways his aunt was thankful when he returned safely each day. Georges was given a short taste of handling a gun himself when the authorities, expecting an attack from White Russian forces backed by a British gunboat far out on the Neva, marched many young boys into a large city square, gave them very hurried and basic rifle training and told them to be ready to defend Petrograd. The boys were frightened to death.

He went almost every day to Theatre Street, hovering about near the school in the hope of a notice announcing its reopening. Many of his student friends were there too; they compared notes, wandered about together and were not above a little discreet looting on their way home. Finally the notice appeared, in spite of an army unit still stationed in the school. An enlightened Bolshevik, Anatole Lunacharsky, who was Commissar for Education, had persuaded Lenin that the opera, ballet and dramatic theatre were not in essence 'decadent'; they were the 'arts of the people', which had been grossly misused by the aristocracy and which the people should now reclaim. And he added, clever man, that the propaganda value of these arts could be as great as that of any industry. So the army moved out, the students and teachers returned and the school and theatre reopened. But it was to be a very different theatre from the ones they remembered in the days of the Tsar.

4
Choreography

Under Bolshevism, performances at the Maryinsky took a strange turn. They became Communist Party meetings with dance interludes. Audiences entered to find the curtain raised on a draped stage, on which prominent party members were seated at a long table while others were in the front rows of the stalls. Speeches and debates continued for several hours while dancers and students waited in the wings, ready to give the hard-pressed public a little of what they had paid for – perhaps the Hindu Dance from *La Bayadère* or a divertissement from *The Nutcracker*. The Hoop Dance, fast and brilliant, was a special favourite. These performances were travesties and the dancers, watching and listening from the wings, were bewildered and depressed. One night Georges heard an abrasive Trotsky in full flow and never forgot the experience.

Gradully full-length performances returned, no doubt through subtle pressure from Anatole Lunacharsky. The Maryinsky was now known as the State Theatre for Opera and Ballet, but the Bolshevik purse was small and there was no money for fuel to heat the theatre, nor for new costumes. With the outside temperature falling to below zero audiences sat in sheepskin coats and boots, stamping their feet to keep their circulation moving, noting the dancers' breath condensing like steam in the cold air. These young people were the lucky ones, doing exactly what Mozart, in his poverty, had done with his Constanza – dancing to keep warm.

Hardship makes for great ingenuity. The students began to

cut up old velvet theatre draperies to make warmer costumes; they became adept at finding scraps of food – when horse lungs or heart could go into a stew it was a red-letter day; and they were given free time from their classes to go and hunt for firewood. Lunacharsky was well aware of their situation and one day, in an attempt to show them that civil war was not exclusively Russian, he took them to a performance of D. W. Griffith's silent film *Birth of a Nation* – translating the English sub-titles for them as the film progressed. Georges always remembered this unusual, humanitarian man with gratitude and affection.

A reminiscence of Georges during these years was given to Bernard Taper by the dancer Vera Kostrovitskaya.

> I remember a slender youth with a fine pale Georgian face, straight dark hair and irreproachably polite and modest manners. He never teased us little ones nor despised us but acted as if we were equals and of the same age, though in those early years a difference of three classes was enormous. Among the students he was noted for his extraordinary understanding of music. He could never pass with indifference by any musical instrument ... the sounds of a piano would be heard ... that would be Balanchivadze improvising or playing the most difficult compositions while waiting for the rehearsal to begin. Sometimes, in the evening, we would secretly climb the stairs to listen to him playing Liszt, Chopin or Beethoven in the boys' quarters above us ... there was no doubt that Balanchivadze was a young man of many talents, though it was not yet clear how his talents would further develop.

Kostrovitskaya, at this time a younger ballet student, later danced in Balanchine's first professional choreographic essays. She describes well the dilemma in which he found himself – whether to continue in the profession for which he had trained so rigorously and successfully, or to go back to the art he loved best, music.

In 1921 he graduated from the school with honours and became a full member of the theatre company. But this only increased his dilemma. He had his own 'revolutionary' ideas about the ballet, believing that the formal and old-fashioned classics which had fitted so well into tsarist life were no longer a reflection of contemporary Russia. He wanted to experiment with much freer, almost acrobatic movement which he felt would not only be more interesting for the public but also more emotionally expressive. He knew that, for so young and un-tested a choreographer, this would be impossible at the State Theatre; so, to clear his mind, he made an unusual decision. While continuing to dance in the corps de ballet he enrolled at the Petrograd Conservatory of Music, studying piano and theory for the next three years.

There was no doubt that music was his first love or that his studies at the Conservatory absorbed and satisfied him. His greatest ambition then – and one encouraged by his father in exuberant letters – was to compose, and for a time he gave it all his energy and concentration. But, blessed with self-perception, he gradually realized that he would never be more than a tolerably good composer. He could have become a notable concert pianist or conductor, but the urge to create rather than to interpret was too strong and so the ballet finally claimed him. At least one celebrated musician was delighted by his choice. 'The world is full of pretty good concert pianists,' Stravinsky said years later, 'but a choreographer such as Balanchine is . . . the rarest of beings.' Interestingly, another great choreographer had experienced similar doubts a few years ealier. Mikhail Fokine, disenchanted with the Maryinsky, had left the ballet to study painting, believing it to be a more worthy profession for a man than mere dancing. He had circulated a questionnaire among the company, and in answer to 'What is the definition of ballet?' one dancer had written, 'Pornography, pure and simple.'

Choreography then, in as new and exciting a guise as he could imagine, was to be Georges' future. He had already made forays into the choreographic field while still a student. Three of his pas de deux had been given at performances in the school theatre. Characteristically, he had called this 'making up dances'. And he was right. His first, at the age of sixteen, was a love duet danced to *La Nuit* for violin and piano by Anton Rubinstein. A member of the school staff was outraged, calling

it 'a scandal of eroticism', and demanded Georges' immediate
dismissal. However the head of the school not only liked it but
was impressed by the boy's initiative, and made it known to the
senior students that a splendid example had been set which he
hoped would be copied. Georges was encouraged; his next
Duet, to Fritz Kreisler's *Schön Rosmarin*, was seen at the
graduation performance, and soon after came another romantic
pas de deux, *Poème*, to music by Zdenek Fibich.

No one who saw *Poème* ever forgot it. Georges danced in it
himself, partnering Shura Danilova. He had designed her costume – a filmy pale blue wisp of material – and he entered from
the wings carrying her 'weightlessly' on his shoulder and arm.
In 1920 this was an astonishing innovation. The ending was
equally effective as Danilova, in a high arabesque, floated away
from the stage held at full arm's height above his head. This was
the birth of the authentic Balanchine touch. *Poème* created
such an effect that the Russian critic Yury Slonimsky, writing in
1975, recalled Vera Kostrovitskaya's memory of Danilova: 'One
had the impression that she herself, without a partner's support, was gliding through the air . . . far, far away'. This pas de
deux was performed at many concerts in the city and suburbs
during the summer, and the public always demanded an
encore.

In 1922 Georges received his first critical review. At the
Music Conservatory he had composed a waltz which he chose
for another Duet, appearing in it himself in a series of dance
programmes at a surburban pavilion. In the 11 June issue of the
Petrograd Theatre and Art News he read, ' . . . on the last night a
special attraction was *Valse*, music and choreography by G. M.
Balanchivadze, executed by A. D. Danilova and the author. The
first name speaks for itself: G. M. Balanchivadze proved to be a
talented composer, choreographer and dancer. Such a combination is a rare one, promising him much in the future.' In fact the
combination was not so much 'a rare one' as unique. Amusingly, the critic Slonimsky took private lessons with Balanchine –
'the better to understand the ballet'. And in New York recently
Clive Barnes told me that he too had toiled at the barre with
another English dance critic, John Percival, in neat little tights
and ballet shoes. ' . . . If you could have seen us!' . . . and this

delightful and comfortably large man broke into wild laughter. But the point is that they *tried*. I like that, and it must surely have increased their understanding – if only of the physical difficulties.

Another event in 1922 remained in Balanchine's memory. For a Red Army charity concert it was announced that the much-loved ballerina Olga Preobrajenska, now over fifty, would be the star attraction. She chose Georges to partner her and they danced an exhilarating Tarantella while the public clapped and cheered. Her payment for this was a loaf of bread. Forty years later Balanchine described her to Bernard Taper: 'She was a little old woman with no neck, like a monkey. It was very nice dancing with her. She had a profound mind. She was like a cardinal.' He had more luck than my own teacher, Nicholas Legat, who often partnered her in her heyday. One night, near the end of a classic ballet, she prepared for a supported pirouette. As she started to spin, her elbow caught Legat full in the mouth. He shut his mouth tight, the ballet finished and the curtain fell. In answer to her: 'Darling, are you all right?' he leaned forward and spat out four teeth and a quantity of blood. Poor Olga fainted clean away!

In the post-Revolution years, without censorship and with tsarist traditions on the wane, experimental art flourished as never before. For creative artists of all kinds the field was clear and they seized their chance greedily. This was the time when the film director Eisenstein made the remarkable *Battleship Potemkin*. Two great experimenters in the world of the dance were Fyodor Lopukhov and Kasyan Goleizovsky, the one based in Petrograd, the other in Moscow.

Lopukhov was the new director and ballet master at the State Theatre; a creative man who was also a good musician, he planned and staged a Dance Symphony, *Grandeur of the Universe*, to the Fourth Symphony of Beethoven. It caused a sensation at its first performance but was torn to shreds by a critic called Akim Volinsky. None of the older traditionalist dancers would take part in the production, but the young ones – Georges among them – loved it. Lopukhov is unknown in the west, sadly, unlike his famous sister Lydia Lopukhova – whose name was changed by Diaghilev to the easier Lopokova. She was tiny and funny, a ballerina of the Ballets Russes and later, improbably and happily the wife of the economist John Maynard Keynes. My last sight of her was at a luncheon party in Sussex; she was in her eighties, wearing a string bag on her head, and accompanied by the Bloomsbury painter Duncan Grant, even older and in carpet slippers.

Though little can be traced of Lopukhov's plotless Dance Symphony, the work of Goleizovsky is still remembered in Russia. He was a dancer-choreographer of great and acknowledged personality. A graduate of the Imperial School, he had gone to Moscow to become an admired leading dancer at the Bolshoi Theatre. But even before the Revolution he had become dissatisfied with the artificiality of the old classics. In place of the extravagant posturings in front of magnificent décors he visualized, as Balanchine did, free-flowing movement with the minimum of adornment. Breaking away to form his own troupe, he embarked on a spectacular series of productions using music by Debussy, Richard Strauss and Scriabin. Goleizovsky was an Impressionist with more than a touch of Diaghilev's magic and Isadora Duncan's unconventionality. He must have seen her on her early Russian tours, when she made such an impact on Fokine. Like her his dancers were barefoot, wore little and moved freely, with abandon. His choice of music, also like hers, was unorthodox. The effect on Georges, when he saw a programme of Goleizovsky's ballets in Petrograd's Hall of Nobles in 1921, was electrifying. He said later that it was Goleizovsky who had given him the courage to try out his most advanced ideas with a small group of young colleagues. This became his first company, with the unsurprising name of The Young Ballet.

Did he know that he too was developing a style of movement pioneered by Isadora Duncan? Probably not – he saw her dance only once, a year later, when Lunacharsky brought her back to Russia at the age of forty-four. She was past her best and undeniably fat, but she still gave recitals. Asked about them later in life, Balanchine's comment was unsurpassingly cruel, 'To me it was absolutely unbelievable – a drunken, fat woman who for hours was rolling around like a pig. It was the most awful thing.' What a tragic dismissal of a woman who had given so much stimulus to the development of dancing through Fokine, Diaghilev, Lopukhov, Goleizovsky and, subsequently, to Balanchine himself.

5
Decision

At the age of eighteen, Georges was now a very attractive young man. He had inherited all the charm and delight in social life of his father Meliton, and some of his lustiness too. In spite of the general hardship of these years he was happy, enjoying all that came his way and basking in his wide popularity with friends of both sexes. His sense of humour and gift for mimicry were great assets, and all the dancers in his young company loved working with him, just as future dancers would throughout his long career.

His zest for life took him into other fields. He staged dances for dramatic plays and operas and appeared in productions of Gluck's *Orpheus and Eurydice* and Stravinsky's *The Nightingale*, directed by Vsevolod Meyerhold, later a famous actor. He made friends with several painters, including Dimitriev, Yakulov and Erbstein, and an unusual dilettante figure, Ivan Sollertinsky; they sat up all night talking, arguing and planning new productions. Georges was particularly interested in the views of Sollertinsky but had some difficulty in understanding them. 'He hurried to say as many words as possible in the shortest time . . . he gasped, stuttered and lisped all at once and all you heard was pshh-pshh-pshh – so it was fascinating to listen to him.'

Salaries at the State Theatre were deplorably low, so many young dancers formed concert groups and gave performances wherever they could get an engagement. Their well-rounded

training proved invaluable – many could sing, play the violin or
piano, or read poetry, so these concerts were delightfully varied
and the public enjoyed them. They travelled to Pavlovsk, a
popular resort near Petrograd, and to Tsarskoe Selo – the Tsar's
Village. There, in the deserted palaces of the Yusopov princes,
Georges' Young Ballet set up house. There were beautiful
gardens and a ballroom with large mirrors, perfect for practising. For the first time in their lives they were free of super-
vision: they had time to stand back and see each other as
attractive young people. Inevitably they fell in love, lived
together and spent a wonderful and idyllic few weeks in the
midst of Russia's travail. Georges' first love was Olga Mung-
alova, a very talented girl who had danced in Lopukhov's
Dance Symphony. In Balanchine's own words to Solomon
Volkov in the 1970s, 'she had exquisitely beautiful legs'. Apart
from this nothing, sadly, is known about her.

Meanwhile there were performances in likely and unlikely
settings including, on several occasions, the circus. Always the
most popular number was a sailors' dance, *Matelot*, written by
Georges for himself, Danilova and another boy, Efimov. 'We
portrayed ship's lads who climbed an imaginary mast and
unfurled sails to polka music. This was not high art, of course,
but we tried to do it merrily and professionally – otherwise we
might not get any food at all.' Sometimes they were paid with a
sack of grain or a haunch of bacon. There might even be a tip – a
few lumps of sugar – which was considered a high honour. The
richest pickings were at the houses of Communist Party
officials, whose larders were filled with food which the Americans were sending to the starving Russian people. One evening
the dancers were rewarded with a succulent piece of liver – the
luxury was almost too much for them.

Georges was now planning and rehearsing for his first Evening of the Young Ballet. It took place on 1 June 1923 in the
Duma, the city parliament on Nevsky Prospect, in a huge hall
with steeply raked seats surrounding the central area – a theatre
in the round. The dancers had no money to advertize their
programme, but the public seemed ready and waiting. That
night the hall was filled to capacity: there was an atmosphere of
excitement and release from tension among the audience,

which brought a crescendo of applause and cheering as the performance ended. The dancers were amazed. Of course the majority of the audience was young; the older ones who had bravely risked the experience left the hall in varying degrees of disapproval, and felt vindicated next day when they read a damning review of the ideas and talents of Balanchivadze. It had been written by the same sour critic, Volinsky, who hated anything untraditional on principle and as early as 1905 had demolished in print the work of Mikhail Fokine.

Foolishly, some months earlier he had opened a choreographic school of his own in Petrograd, presumably to preserve the culture he imagined that he alone understood. Thus he laid himself wide open to attack. After the slashing censure of the Young Ballet Georges was unable to resist a counter-blast. He wrote an amusing and malicious article about this school under the title 'How Mr Volinsky Flogged Himself' – a quote adapted from Gogol's *Inspector General* – which was printed in the magazine *Teatr*, with a large photograph of Georges on the cover. The article caused quite a stir and for some weeks he was the artistic talk of Petrograd.

But now his mind was on other things. He had discovered that he was attractive to women – most women, it seemed. He cultivated a soulful Chopinesque appearance – deathly pale skin, dark, hollow eyes, black hair combed to fall interestingly forward and then to be swept back with a pale, fragile hand. He practised a brooding look and would haunt prominent parts of the city where he knew he would be seen. His eyes were indeed wonderful, and several dancers were convinced that the make-up pot had been brought into play. This splendid pose might have continued to dazzle the female population but for his sense of humour, which constantly got the better of him. One evening at the State Theatre, as Bernard Taper recounts, he had a small solo rôle as a tramp in the ballet *Esmeralda*. He made himself up as a short man with a large head, long hair falling from the crown and a little goatee beard; on his entrance he fussed about the stage with the quaintest of mannerisms. He had transformed himself into a living replica of the artistic director of the theatre, Mr V. P. Rapoport. The company was convulsed and barely able to dance. Rapoport, as it happened, was in the auditorium that night, but he also had a sense of humour and issued no reprimand of any kind. By this time the Chopinesque look was increasingly difficult to sustain.

A young girl, fair-haired and attractive, came to evening classes at the ballet school. Her name was Tamara Zheverzheyeva, later abbreviated to Geva, and Georges met her by chance one evening at her ballroom dancing class. Soon he was seeing her often: they started to take engagements together at little nightclubs, she singing in a light, cabaret-style voice, he accompanying her at the piano. She took him home to meet her very rich father. Zheverzheyev lived in an enormous house in Grafskiy Alley where he kept his huge collection of books, including hundreds of first editions. He owned a brocade mill and a church supply store on Nevsky Prospect, and had built his own theatre in Troytskaya Street. He also possessed a beautiful grand piano; Georges was thus particularly welcome. Zheverzheyev, perhaps unfortunately, was very fond of Wagner, and when Georges arrived to take Tamara out he would be waiting for him. 'Do please sit down and play something of Wagner's,' he would say, and there would be the *Tristan* or *Tannhäuser* score ready on the piano. What could Georges do? While Tamara waited in another room, Georges would play . . . and play. Wagner is nothing if not long-winded, and Zheverzheyev loved every second. 'Oh, you *can't* leave before this bit – just a little more.' Sometimes a whole hour passed in this way, and to the end of his life Balanchine couldn't stand Wagner.

A story has been told many times – indeed by Tamara herself – of how one day her father said to Georges, 'Now look here, you children, why don't you two get married?' It comes into her autobiography *Split Seconds*, which though vivid and interesting at moments has more than a whiff of a romantic novel. Balanchine himself, talking to Solomon Volkov in 1982, was quite definite. 'Zheverzheyev demanded Wagner from me, that's true. But to marry Tamara, no. Tamara and I got married on our own.' And so they did. They were both ridiculously young and seem to have treated such a major decision as a bit of a lark.

The years 1923 and 1924 were hectic ones for Georges, who

was not only working intensively with his Young Ballet, but also taking on many outside commissions. He danced regularly at the State Theatre and played the piano for rehearsals three hours a day to augment his salary. He arranged dances for several plays, Shaw's *Caesar and Cleopatra* among them, he staged a mime performance of Darius Milhaud's *Boeuf sur le Toît*, he arranged a strange choreography of movement-to-poetry for a cabaret called *The Carousel*, and became ballet master at the Maly Opera House where he arranged the dances for Rimsky-Korsakov's *Coq d'Or*. This astonishing pitch of activity came quite naturally to him; the more work he accepted, the more his invention flowed and the greater his energy – Balanchine kept this marvellous facility all his life.

But, though he was so much in demand, everything was not well. He was facing more and more opposition from the older public, the critics and now the authorities, who felt his Evenings of the Young Ballet posed some kind of subversive threat to their ideas of Russian culture. The State Theatre started to apply pressure and to oppose their dancers who were also working with him. At first this was taken lightly and the concert performances continued, but gradually Georges realized that his little company was doomed. He became increasingly irritated by the restricted atmosphere of Petrograd and his thoughts started to stray towards western Europe. He had no real knowledge of the artistic situation abroad, but the idea of open, free societies, untouched by revolution and its aftermath, attracted him strongly. He was only on the brink of such thoughts when a comparatively small episode at the State Theatre pushed him over the edge.

He had become interested in Stravinsky's score *Pulcinella*, and he and his friend Dimitriev, the painter, went to see Lopukhov with plans for a production. Much animated discussion took place, for Lopukhov always enjoyed their company, and the general impression given to the two young men was more than favourable. A few days later everything had changed. They were told that there were problems in the use of the score: Stravinsky was abroad, and the theatre would have to pay him in hard currency; of course there was none available, so there could be no *Pulcinella*. A year later Balanchine heard that

Pulcinella had indeed been staged – by Lopukhov and, to his
sorrow, Dimitriev. He gave a typical quote to Solomon Volkov
about this, *à la* Nikita Khrushchev: 'There wasn't room in the
church for an apple to fall. The Mayor came in – and room was
found.' It is from Gogol.

Even without this fore-knowledge he was now determined to
leave Russia, and discovered that Tamara and several other
dancers were anxious to do the same. By sheer chance, Georges
met Vladimir Dimitriev – no relation of the painter. Dimitriev
had been a baritone with the old Maryinsky Opera and now
worked as a croupier in a government gambling casino. He had
a knack of making friends with high Communist officials – and
keeping on their right side – and he had contrived to salt away
some useful foreign exchange. Privately he wanted to leave
Russia and, through his interest in the dancers, he was able to
arrange for five of them, with three singers, a conductor and
himself, to make a short European tour as the Soviet State
Dancers. It was almost too good to be true.

Georges, Tamara, Shura Danilova and Nicholas Efimov were
four of the group and an exceptionally talented and beautiful
girl, Lydia Ivanova, was to be the fifth. She had attracted much
attention at the State Theatre, had danced with the Young
Ballet and was also a charming singer whom Georges had
accompanied many times at concerts. She had become a
favourite with various Party men: Georges remembered one
particular admirer, a member of the Cheka – the Bolshevik
secret police. 'He always took trouble with us, wined and dined
us, spent a lot of time with us. I remember he used to kiss
Lydia's shoulders. He had an affair with her – not love, just a
balletomane intrigue. It's so easy, after all!'

Danilova's memories go further. At this time she remembers a
young government official, pale and trembling, hanging about
in the theatre corridors. The dancers were sure that he was a
spy. She remembers Lydia coming to a concert one evening
after a visit to a fortune-teller, a well-known weakness of theatre
people. Having put her ring into a glass of wine, the gipsy had
told her to beware of water. So Lydia told Shura that she
couldn't go abroad with the group. Yet a few days later she
accepted an invitation from her secret policeman for a boat trip

on a large lake – just the two of them and three other government officials. A heavy lake paddle-steamer came straight
towards them; it never changed course, hitting the little boat
fair and square and smashing it to pieces. All four men were
picked up, but not Lydia. Balanchine always remained convinced that she knew something too sensitive, that the accident
was prearranged. 'And then,' he told Volkov, 'Lydia was a
marvellous swimmer.'

Shaken, the now smaller group gathered on the quay beside
the German steamer which would take them across the Baltic to
Stettin. Dimitriev was with them – it was as if they were going
on a simple holiday tour, but further afield than usual. Not a
word was spoken, though each head carried the same thought.
There were heart-stopping delays with officials and papers but
at last they walked up the gangplank and on board. More delays
– would the red tape never end? Finally the engines turned and
the ship moved slowly out on the water, but the tension among
the dancers lasted until they were well clear of the naval guns at
Kronstadt. Then they relaxed. A few of those young people
would never see their families or their homeland again.

Part 2

6
Diaghilev

All dancers share one characteristic. When we are not straining
at our work, when we are at home, at parties or travelling, there
is one simple, over-riding desire – food. As soon as the German
steamer sailed into the open sea Georges, Tamara, Shura and
Efimov ran down the stairs to the dining room. It was an
unforgettable moment for them, as Balanchine told Bernard
Taper a half century later: 'It was such a beautiful sight – all that
beautiful bread just sitting there, like that, so casually, with
nobody guarding it – that I almost wept.'

After all they had been through the four days' voyage seemed
Elysian, but arriving in Berlin brought back reality. There was
very little money and no engagement for the tiny company. It
was the height of summer and most Berliners were on holiday,
leaving the city with the air of a perpetual Sunday. Berlin was a
dreary, dowdy place in 1924, but these young Russians found it
the epitome of chic. They bought clothes, and they had their
hair cut in the western way, then bought more clothes and
watched their money dwindle.

Within their first ten days of freedom a telegram arrived from
the authorities in Russia demanding their immediate return.
Conductor, singers and dancers – Dimitriev gathered them all
together to face this ultimatum. For the conductor and singers
there seemed to be no problem – they would return at once. But
for the dancers and Dimitriev himself? They must have been
greatly torn between their own country and families and their

longing for the private and professional freedom offered by western Europe. They all chose the latter, with no regrets then or later – surely a triumph of fatalistic hope. Balanchine always retained this wonderfully optimistic view of life – always looking forwards even from the gloomiest present. He was able to bring the same attitude to bear on all his own work. Ballets were good or not so good at any given time; depending on the human material at his disposal he would change and rework the choreography of even his most celebrated ballets, for he had no false pride about his original creation. He loved to experiment, to think afresh – a singular trait among choreographers.

Now Dimitriev showed his metal, having at last succeeded in arranging a tour of resorts in the Rhineland during the late summer months. The performances cannot have been good, as production and décor were almost non-existent, but the little group kept its head above water while Dimitriev searched unceasingly for new contacts and new engagements. Surprisingly, from his base in Berlin the new contract he secured was in London – a spot on the variety bill at the Empire Theatre, Leicester Square. This proved a disaster both for performers and management: apart from their slightly inappropriate repertoire of solos and pas de deux, the dancers were quite unable to cope with the high-speed changes of costume required in a variety show. They survived for two weeks, and then their contracts and work permits came to an end.

It was early in November when they returned across the Channel to France, making their way to Paris and finding cheap rooms in a little hotel in the place de la République. Their situation was now very precarious – the days passed and no work came their way. Tamara, Shura and Efimov became worried and depressed, but not Georges. He was calm and sanguine, as certain as Mr Micawber that something would turn up. And it did, in the shape of a telegram from Sergey Pavlovich Diaghilev.

Always on the lookout for new talent from Russia, Diaghilev had tracked them down to their drab hotel. The telegram asked them to come next day to the salon of his great friend and patron, Misia Sert, to audition for him. Diaghilev was almost unknown to these young people; they had heard his name in

Russia, had heard that he had a company somewhere – and that was all. Indeed, Shura Danilova was rather put out at the idea of having to audition for anyone. Having danced with distinction at the Maryinsky, she felt this to be recommendation enough. But the quartet was in such straits that this was no time for a flourish of ego; they all arrived at the rendezvous in good time, thankful to have the prospect of dancing again.

The man who waited for them was the *grand seigneur* of the ballet, perhaps of all theatre, as his influence embraced everyone working in the performing arts. Born in 1872 in the Selistchev barracks in the province of Novgorod where his father was an officer of the Imperial Guard, he had spent his first eighteen years in the country. His twenty-two-year-old mother had died a few days after his birth and, when his father married again, his stepmother was, in Diaghilev's words, 'the best woman in the world'. She taught him to love literature and music; he was a good pianist by the age of twelve. An aunt, who was an excellent singer, had songs written for her by Tchaikovsky, who was a family friend, and Diaghilev came to love and revere him. Also in their house, from time to time, appeared an unassuming little man with sheets of music spilling from a tattered cardigan – his aunt's occasional accompanist, Modest Mussorgsky.

In 1890, aged eighteen, he arrived in St Petersburg to take, unwillingly, a law degree at the University and, willingly, a music degree at the Conservatory. He had a good baritone voice but his talent was not enough for a professional career and he showed the same self-perception that Georges had shown when he gave up composition. But something of real importance happened to Daighilev at this time. He was introduced by a cousin into a small, select group of revolutionary artists led by Alexandre Benois (the great-uncle of Peter Ustinov) and a dapper, red-haired Jew called Rosenberg who was already startling the art world under his assumed name of Léon Bakst. They thought Diaghilev a country bumpkin: Benois took over his 'artistic' education and within a couple of years was outstripped by his pupil. Painting had become a focal point in Daighilev's life.

It is a universal belief that the ballet was the abiding passion of this remarkable man – any mention of his name brings the invariable response, 'Ballets Russes.' But, surprisingly, it was not so. He had three artistic passions – music, painting and literature. Literature would assert itself towards the end of his life, fuelled by his beloved Pushkin – the most Russian of writers for Russians, even though he was in fact part African! But Diaghilev's great work was built on music and painting.

As a young man, under the tutelage of Benois and Bakst, he travelled throughout Europe studying Florentine and Venetian art, then the French, German, Scandinavian and English schools. He mounted exhibitions in Russia; he won the Uvarov Prize from the Academy of Sciences for a monograph, and in 1905 he showed Russians their history and heritage in an amazing exhibition of portraits amassed from the entire Empire. His travels took him to Yasnaya Polyana, the estate of Leo Tolstoy, where he said he was 'awed and silent in the presence of the great writer'. With this exhibition Diaghilev discovered his own flair as an impresario. He had chosen to show it in the huge Tavrida Palace in St Petersburg, which had been standing empty and useless until he realized its possibilities as an art gallery. He took part of this exhibition to Paris in 1906, to the Salle d'Automne in the Grand Palais where, with Léon Bakst, he transformed ordinary galleries into gold-brocaded rooms and trellised winter gardens. From the beginning he knew the secret – that the setting and the way you present something to the public is as important as anything you choose to present.

Diaghilev had great charm – he collected patrons with consummate ease. The following year he was back in Paris with a series of Russian concerts in which several composers – Rimsky-Korsakov, Glazunov and Rachmaninov – conducted their own works. In 1908 he brought the bass Fyodor Chaliapin in Mussorgsky's *Boris Godunov* to the Paris Opéra. The magnificent Slavic settings were designed by Golovine and Benois, the costumes by Bilibine – and these, with the intensely Russian music and Chaliapin at the peak of his powers, caused a sensation. Diaghilev was delighted but not entirely satisfied: something was missing, something that opera alone could not provide.

For many years he had been a devoted follower of the

Maryinsky company: he had watched Fokine, Nijinsky, Pavlova and Karsavina graduate from the school and blossom as professional performers. He had even held an administrative post in the theatre for a few years, when he had edited the *Imperial Theatre Year Book* — beautifully and expensively, but not entirely happily. Now, at the end of the Paris Opéra season, he and a few close friends met for a celebratory dinner. In the group was a former music publisher, now an impresario working closely with Diaghilev — a wiry, witty little Frenchman called Gabriel Astruc. Almost unknown today, Astruc had the original idea for the first Ballets Russes season and was largely responsible for its creation; and it happened at this dinner party.

They were discussing *Boris Godunov* and Astruc began to rhapsodize about the setting and production of the Polish Act III and particularly the dancing of the Polonaise by members of the Maryinsky corps de ballet. Diaghilev then described the glories of the Maryinsky — 'the divine Pavlova', Nijinsky, 'the lion of the dance', and the young choreographer of genius, Mikhail Fokine. Astruc, greatly excited by this, declared, 'I shall bring them all to Paris next season.' Diaghilev had grave doubts; he felt that western Europe was not yet ready for complete evenings of ballet, and he tried to dissuade the by now impassioned Astruc. He failed: the next morning Astruc had a contract for the non-existent company drawn up and ready for signature and then, with typical French panache, he was at the door of every rich patron of the arts to secure enough backing for the venture. Diaghilev now had the formidable task — but one he relished — of creating the Ballets Russes from all the talent of St Petersburg.

So in 1909, with his famous first season, Diaghilev achieved what he now knew he had always wanted — the fusion of music and painting through the medium of the ballet. Blessed with faultless artistic taste, he supervized every detail of each production, lighting many of them himself; his theatrical vision was so far-reaching that he was often years ahead of his public — in Balanchine's view 'twenty-five years ahead'. Another invaluable gift, never matched by anyone since, was his ability to recognize, secure and nurture raw, early talent in all artistic

fields, both creative and interpretative – the career of Igor
Stravinsky, given his first important commission by Diaghilev,
is a perfect example. This, then, was the man who sat waiting in
Misia Sert's Paris salon in 1924, hoping that once again he
might find someone unique.

When the young dancers arrived, who did they see? Jean
Cocteau has left a graphic description of Diaghilev at this time:

> His dancers called him Chinchilla because of a white streak in
> his hair, which was dyed deep black. He wrapped himself in a
> pelisse with an opossum collar and sometimes fastened it with
> safety pins. He had the face of a bulldog and the smile of a baby
> crocodile, with one tooth sticking outside. If he ground his teeth
> it was a sign of pleasure, fear or anger . . . And his moist eyes as
> they looked downwards were curved like Portuguese oysters.

After the audition Diaghilev asked Georges if he could make
opera ballets 'very fast' and received the reply, 'very fast',
though in fact he had only tried his hand at this once in Russia.
Nothing further was said and the group returned to their hotel,
waiting disconsolately for several days without news. Then
word came – an offer for all four to join the Ballets Russes
during its current London season, which they accepted more
gratefully than Diaghilev could know.

Soon after their arrival at the London Coliseum, Diaghilev
sent a message. A number of dancers would be free for a whole
day and he wanted Georges to demonstrate more of his choreographic skill. For Georges, who had been engaged solely as a
dancer, it was the perfect opportunity. Everyone gathered in the
studio of a well-known teacher, Serafina Astafieva, and among
the dancers was a young Irish girl, Edris Stannus, who, for her
profession, had chosen the name of a line of French kings –
Ninette de Valois. Daighilev hated this: refusing to accept it, he
always wrote 'Devalois'!

She has clear memories of that day and of the impression
created by the young, would-be ballet master. 'He was just a boy –
such a boy,' but one who immediately gained respect by his
quiet, purposeful manner and complete professionalism. He
taught them his arrangement of Chopin's *Marche Funèbre* and

in the afternoon Diaghilev arrived to see it. He sat wrapped in his opossum-collared coat, monocle in place, taking in every detail but with an expressionless face. 'Oh, he just sat there, impassive as usual – looking like a piece of liver,' was Ninette's comment; I forgot to ask her whether cooked or uncooked. When the *Marche* ended there was silence. Diaghilev rose and, without a word, left the studio. No one knew if this meant success or disaster.

In 1924, Diaghilev's only choreographer was Bronislava Nijinska, sister of Vaslav. She was a talented woman and had choreographed several notable ballets, but her relationship with Diaghilev was not happy and the company knew that he was anxious to replace her. Her uncomfortable situation was made considerably worse when the twenty-six-year-old Georges appeared on the scene. 'Nijinska was absolutely beastly to him,' said Ninette with a laugh. Matters came to a head during the remainder of the Coliseum season, and before it ended Diaghilev made an announcement: Bronislava Nijinska would be leaving the company, and the new choreographer would be Georges Balanchine. The impresario, whose company worked mainly in France, had decided that the new name would be more appropriate and certainly more pronounceable. Presumably the recipient quite liked it too.

7
Ballets Russes

In 1924, after many years of wandering, the Ballets Russes had at last found a home. With the help of a patron, the Princess of Monaco, the company was affiliated to the opera in the Principality; hence the necessity to have a choreographer who could make opera ballets 'very fast'. There were short ballet seasons in the miniature Monte Carlo theatre and also in Paris and London, but Balanchine's main task in the mid-twenties, and a most unrewarding one, was to inject life into the tired old dances traditionally required in so many operas. For dancers the worst fate is dancing in these operas – for orchestral musicians the worst fate is playing for the ballet.

Ninette de Valois remembers with pleasure the miracle wrought by the new 'Balanchine' on this wretched scenario. She found him brilliant, funny, intelligent and strongly individualistic. The company, at first nonplussed at having someone so young in this authorative position, soon warmed to his easy-going, amusing manner and to his courtesy – a great contrast to the temperamental behaviour of earlier choreographers. They had previously been subjected to Fokine with his passionate rages and his habit of throwing around anything that came to hand, even a dancer. They had suffered under poor, distracted Nijinsky when he was being destroyed by the homosexual demands of Diaghilev upon his basically heterosexual nature. Then they had to endure Diaghilev's greatest love, Léonide Miassin – later known as Massine – who brooded blackly in the same situation and then ran off with an English dancer, Vera Clarke (known as Vera Savina in the Ballets Russes), the first of his tally of wives. The great impresario had never made any bones about his homosexuality, and it was common knowledge to many of the public, who came to accept it as part and parcel of the strange, unreal world of the ballet. They were not wrong. I cannot adequately describe the delighted shock, for at least one female dancer, on discovering that a passing Prince Siegfried or Count Albrecht was a normal, full-blooded male. The difference that this could make to one's stage performance was very great – but it was all too infrequent.

Diaghilev arranged the repertoire of the Ballets Russes for the favourite of the moment. There were the Nijinsky years, then the Massine years, the ballets and the casting reflecting the personal relationship. Now, in 1925, it was the reign of Serge Lifar – a splendid *beau gosse* in his golden youth who gradually became extravagantly flamboyant and, later, none too accurate of memory. And there was Georges – married, different, but essential.

Within the first five months of that year he choreographed sixteen productions: solos; pas de deux, trois, quatres; and dances for four, six, eight, twelve couples – in operas ranging from Bizet's *Carmen* through Massenet's *Thaïs* and *Manon* and Mussorgsky's *Fair at Sorotchinsk* to the interestingly titled *Fay-Yen-Fah* in three acts by Joseph Redding. These are labours of Hercules which the public can never fully realize and appreciate, yet to each one he brought energy and unsurpassed invention. Ninette spoke of a pas de trois – she cannot now remember the opera – which he arranged for Danilova, Lubov Tchenicheva and herself. 'It was perfectly beautiful,' she recalled, and the expression on her face showed it to be true. She also spoke with particular admiration of his staging of Maurice Ravel's *L'Enfant et les Sortilèges*, Balanchine's first major work for Diaghilev. Described on the programme as a Lyric Fantasy, his production gave the dancers equality with the singers for the first time and this was highly successful. Everyone who remembers it speaks of the originality of the conception. The libretto was by Colette, the décor and costumes

by Alphonse Visconti and Georgette Vialet, and the conductor
was Victor de Sabata.

Balanchine would make three more stagings of this work in
future years, always with fresh invention and renewed success,
but – and this is odd in such an accomplished musician – in
1925 he was quite unaware of Ravel as an exceptional master of
orchestration. This was an increasing regret which nagged at
him over many years until, in 1975, he finally resolved it for
himself, to the surprise of his, by then staunch American
public.

Listening to Ninette de Valois talking of those early days in
Monte Carlo, I felt less sure about the validity of some of her
further statements: 'Diaghilev never really liked Balanchine
and never appreciated him'; 'Balanchine refused to be educated
by Diaghilev'; and how his lack of taste in décor and costume
'was always hopeless – he was quite uninterested'. There is
some truth in this last comment. Balanchine's decorative vision
was always weak, and many of his ballets were marred by
unsuitable or ugly décor and dresses. But, far from refusing
Diaghilev's education, he admitted that he learnt a great deal
from him, willingly and with appreciation. The impresario
loved to instruct and to give his protégés the opportunity to
become as artistically cultivated as himself. In 1925 he visited
many of his favourite galleries and museums in Italy with Serge
Lifar, Boris Kochno, his young secretary and librettist, and
Georges. He also recommended certain books, and every evening was spent discussing various aspects of art. With such a
guide it would have been impossible to remain untouched by
this experience, and Balanchine later wrote, 'It is because of
Diaghilev that I am whatever I am today.' This, I am sure, is also
inaccurate; it is so easy to exaggerate in retrospect, we all do it.
But certainly Balanchine's career was dramatically altered by
his years with the Ballets Russes, and his feeling of indebted-
ness to Diaghilev was profound and genuine.

The early months of 1925 also included a journey to London
where Georges, with Diaghilev, visited Astafieva's studio to see
a talented fourteen-year-old called Alice Marks, soon to be
Alicia Markova. Her technique was astonishing for her age.
Georges was asked to put her through her paces, which he did

with admiration and amusement. After two hours he was certain that she was the right dancer for the rôle of the Nightingale in his first full-length ballet, *Le Chant du Rossignol*, to music by Stravinsky and with setting and costumes by Matisse. An earlier production choreographed by Massine and with Karsavina in the title role had been unsuccessful and withdrawn from the repertoire. Now, for a new and more lyrical production, this quiet, precocious child was shipped across to Monte Carlo, with a governess, for the start of an exceptional career.

Balanchine and Stravinsky were to become such celebrated collaborators that it is tempting to see in the *Rossignol* some special and glorious beginning. But it wasn't so – it was a slight work, interesting and inventive but chiefly memorable for the début of the tiny, frail Markova. She loved working with Georges, who was only a few years older than herself; she found him funny, light-hearted, and very clear and exact in rehearsals. Diaghilev was very fond of her and even had thoughts of adopting her. She told me that she called him 'Sergey-pop', which I find comically touching. In spite of the *Rossignol* being very much her ballet, its most notorious performance was one in which she did not take part.

Some months after the first performance she fell ill shortly before the rise of the curtain. Pandemonium! Who knew the part – who could take her place? It was soon clear that only Georges knew the choreography and, though he protested noisily, Diaghilev insisted that he should appear. Markova's costume was like a pocket handkerchief, so Karsavina's old white one, covered in cabbage-sized white roses, was fished out of a wardrobe skip; Georges poured himself into it, whitened his face and prepared to perform. In the ballet the Nightingale makes her first entrance carried to centre stage in a cage; Markova had looked like a little, delicate bird – Balanchine, in his own words, 'like a gorilla'. 'A stuffed rabbit' was the verdict of Pavel Tchelitchev, a designer working with the company, who was in the audience. Georges' performance was, in fact, rather good, his gift for mimicry giving a strong flavour of the fourteen-year-old and her 'way' with his choreography; but everyone on the stage, as well as Diaghilev in his box, was so

convulsed with suppressed laughter that the quality of his
performance went almost unnoticed. It was, as critics like to
say, the definitive rendering, and a moment of spice and
ribaldry which all performers secretly adore.

Ribaldry is the right word for the second full-length ballet
which Balanchine made for the company. *Barabau*, to music by
the young, unknown Vittorio Rieti and settings by Utrillo, was
based on an old Italian nursery song and was, in Boris Kochno's
phrase, 'Italian buffoonery'. It was given its première at the
London Coliseum in December 1925. The English did not like
it – they expected from Diaghilev an unbroken chain of *Fire-
birds* and *Shéhérazades*, nostalgia playing its usual part in the
public imagination. The dancers wore false noses and padded
bosoms and bottoms; it was real knockabout stuff, causing the
English critic Cyril Beaumont to write, 'This is merely vulgar
and rather tedious . . . *Barabau* fills me with misgivings as to
the wisdom of Diaghilev's choice of Balanchine as choreographer.' Europeans, by comparison, loved the ballet and signalled their appreciation rousingly.

Barabau was not a great work but it is a reminder of
Balanchine's youth and *joie de vivre*. He was a very 'young'
young man: he loved Monte Carlo, loved living in the sun, lying
on the beach, eating delicious meals, doing the work he
enjoyed – even the dreaded operas. He was happy enough with
Tamara but he viewed their marriage as lightly as she did – it
was not, after all, a grand passion. He got into one or two
scrapes. Diaghilev caught him cutting morning rehearsals to get
out of a dreary studio and into the sunshine, and that lapse was
not to be repeated. But Georges was incapable of curbing his
sense of the ridiculous on stage.

He danced in many ballets in the repertoire, giving enormous
pleasure to the company and causing some stress to the
management. In Stravinsky's *Petrushka*, on a balcony an excited peasant was seen waving his legs and feet instead of his
arms – Georges. In Rossini's *La Boutique Fantasque*, one winter
season, a character in the Mazurka appeared covered in green
whiskers from top to toe like a Christmas tree – Georges.
Sometimes, when he appeared as the evil wizard, Kastchei, in
Stravinsky's *Firebird*, he was unable to resist burlesque and, as

audience laughter grew, Diaghilev would hurry backstage with a reprimand.

Ninette de Valois remembers him in company classes – 'He was always at the back, giggling and messing around' – and she speaks of an occasion in Paris when the Opéra director gave a eulogy of Georges to the full company while the subject stood slightly behind him, pulling faces and making ridiculous gestures. As for his dancing, 'It was terrible!', she says scathingly, but Alicia Markova has a different view. 'He was a wonderful dancer,' she says, quite unequivocally. 'He had such elegance and he was a marvellous partner, showing off his ballerina so beautifully.' She remembers this from his many performances as the Prince in Act III of *The Sleeping Beauty*, which the Ballets Russes gave as *Aurora's Wedding*. Best of all was his dancing of the Lezghinka – a famous Georgian folk dance. Not only Alicia but Tamara Geva and Shura Danilova speak of this as 'unforgettable' – he danced it *à trois* with Lubov Tchernicheva and a vigorous Polish character dancer, Léon Woizikovsky.

Apparently impervious to criticism of his choreography, he minded passionately if his dancing was criticized. He believed he was a good dancer and he took pride in his ability and performance. I have only seen him dance once – on film which was old, grainy, a little fast and jerky. With him were Lopokova and Anton Dolin, but I didn't see them – my eyes were rivetted on Balanchine. This was not deliberate: I couldn't help it. He had all the qualities which excite me most – style, speed, dash and élan. And he looked terrific. Danilova speaks of his elevation – 'He could jump like a flea' – and Tamara Geva cites his performance in the Hoop Dance from the *Nutcracker*, when, she says, he and the hoops became, 'a whirling mass . . . he never seemed to touch the ground'.

There was one other area in which Balanchine disliked any breath of criticism – his cooking! He always remembered his mother's delicious food, but it was the French cooking in Monte Carlo which turned him into an excellent chef. He loved experimenting and inventing and soon became quite expert. One evening he invited Diaghilev to dinner, but then became nervous and the preparations did not go smoothly. Danilova was another guest and, though she cannot now remember the

first two courses, she says they were 'complicated' and 'a
disaster'. 'Are you trying to poison me?' said Diaghilev, not
altogether jokingly. Then the pudding arrived – a miracle of
whole apples, the centres filled with chopped nuts, baked in
light mille-feuilles pastry with lashings of thick, fresh cream. It
was superb and Georges had redeemed himself. Until the last
year of his life he found the greatest pleasure and relaxation in
cooking, producing delicious suppers for his various wives
when they returned exhausted from the theatre. What a gift in a
husband!

As he grew older, Balanchine liked to use the creation of
dishes and the composition of a menu as an analogy for his
creation of ballets and the composition of a programme. It could
be very apt. In an article he wrote for *Playbill* in December
1957, when the New York City Ballet was almost ten years old,
he said:

A resident ballet company has to provide an habitual repertory,
like an opera-house, but with the difference that ballet repertory
must offer more than half its programme as absolute novelties . . .
As manager of the restaurant, I am responsible for the menu of
four ballets in an evening.

On a programme the analogy cannot be pressed too far. I do not
pretend that the first ballet on a programme is hors d'oeuvres,
although late-comers tend to make us think so. No choreographer, including me, likes to have a careful composition
considered as a perfunctory opener, but there are certain smaller
or more quiet works which seem appropriate to start a programme, just as there are other, large and brilliant, which serve to
close an evening with brio and splendour. But when I am
cooking up a new season, as I have been now for the last six
months, one has to consider the balance of taste: the relative
lightness or heaviness of the dishes, the time allowed for cooking
(as little union overtime as possible), as well as a discreet or
piquant mixture, flavour and surprise. Unlike chefs, who can
make their choice of an undemanding leek, a modest pepper or a
passive roast, balletmasters realise that a ballerina requires more
than basting: she always wants new ballets, handmade to her
measure, personal style, quality, and quite unlike anything
tasted on land or sea before.

After a short description of a new ballet, *Agon*, he wrote that Stravinsky's music was 'tasty, eatable, digestible and memorable. After hearing its score some hundred times. I still smack my lips. . .it is a masterpiece by a genuine cordon bleu composer.' In the article's final paragraph he wrote:

All recipes are not as involved as the construction of a Swiss watch. I am an old hand at a big casserole which some of my critics have called applause machines. In managing a large restaurant, there are also the desserts, the parfaits, the banana royals and the peach melbas. Calculated vulgarity is a very useful ingredient, but you even have to know how to salt and pepper mere ham and eggs.

Through these quietly amusing comparisons, Balanchine frequently brought many members of the public to a better understanding of the construction and aims of his ballets.

Despite the lotus life of Monte Carlo, Diaghilev's dancers were poor. Their salaries were basic – advances were necessary each month, and many of the company lived in a permanent state of debt to the management. For Georges and his three colleagues there was also the question of Dimitriev, to whom they owed so much. They had made an agreement with him before leaving Russia and this they honoured, paying him commission on every pay cheque received during these years. So gambling and the high life of the Principality were hardly a problem for them.

The Casino, virtually in the same building as the theatre, had been placed out of bounds to the company after a spree by Chaliapin some years earlier when he had lost his head and his full season's salary at the tables. Even so, an occasional dancer strayed into the white and gold rooms and one evening Georges, with his last twenty francs in his pocket, decided to risk the lot. He was twenty-two and had never gambled before; he wandered up to a table, put everything on number thirteen and then, feeling rather foolish, turned to leave. He was at the door when the wheel stopped spinning, he heard shouts and an official hurried towards him. He had been lucky, his winnings were – to him – considerable, so he spent a much more comfortable month than usual – and he never gambled again.

This story is amusingly similar to my own single gambling experience, in the same Casino, possibly in the same room at the same table. In 1947 I was finishing a gruelling week of location work for the film *The Red Shoes* and on our last night the actor Marius Goring decided that I couldn't fly back to London without sampling the Casino. In we went, collected our chips, found a table and, with a shaking hand, I put the whole lot on number three. The next moment a mountain of chips was pushed towards me, all of which I dropped on the way to the cash desk. I had won twenty pounds and was so over-excited that Marius walked me round and round the gardens in the square until I calmed down. I was twenty-one and, like Balanchine, I have never risked my luck since.

In the early months of 1926 the opera ballets continued, seven very different productions and all successful enough to bring audiences to the Opera House for the dancing rather than the music. This was Diaghilev's bread and butter, while his main preoccupation was always new painters, new composers, and new styles of choreography for new and original full-length ballets. During the twenty years of his Ballets Russes, Diaghilev was always the centre of European artistic activity. With his immense taste and his theatrical flair he could command the services of any composer and painter he wanted. His productions, even the less successful ones, carried such prestige that everyone, whether celebrated or unknown, longed to work with him. He could give them all a unique showcase for their talents. But he was now ageing and suffering greatly from diabetes, which he aggravated by a crass disregard for medical advice. His health affected his judgement, and occasionally he mounted productions which were merely slick and clever. Georges became part of this phase – he saw what Diaghilev wanted and, with his willingness to try anything, wrote three ballets that year which were received with a mixture of mild approval, irritation and downright disgust. It would be fascinating to know if Balanchine's direction would have been radically different without the 'modish' influence of Diaghilev.

First he made a 'semi-production', inserting an Entr'acte into a ballet by Nijinska, *Romeo and Juliet*, with a score by the

twenty-year-old Constant Lambert, a setting by the surrealist
Max Ernst and a front curtain by Juan Miró. It was a strange
piece, having little to do with Shakespeare and everything to do
with a theatre company in rehearsal, the two leading players
being in love and, far from dying together, eloping in an
aeroplane. Balanchine's contribution was to raise the front
curtain approximately three feet for his Entr'acte and to choreograph solely for the legs of the characters on the stage. This can
be a surprisingly effective device, as I know from a film made
by Alexander Korda in which I took part called *The Man who
Loved Redheads*, adapted by Terence Rattigan from his play
Who is Sylvia? To demonstrate the passage of time Korda
wanted me to impersonate five young women arriving on the
hero's doorstep with only their legs visible, but with each
personality clearly defined. I have rarely enjoyed a film
sequence more – the shy, hesitant one, the furious one rushing
out of the house and kicking the door, the 'bopping' twenties'
flapper, and so on. The sequence won an award in America and
I still have a startling piece of cubist metal on a little plinth
somewhere in a cupboard.

La Pastorale, Jack in the Box and *The Triumph of Neptune*
were Balanchine's principal productions in 1926, the first two
ballets premièred at the Théâtre Sarah Bernhardt in Paris and
the third in London at the Lyceum. *Pastorale* had the silliest of
stories by Kochno – a film company comes to a country
meadow on location, a young telegraph boy rides by on his
bicycle, is ensnared by the star and dallies; the furious villagers
arrive demanding their mail, whereupon the telegraph boy
rides off! The music by Georges Auric and the décor by Pruna
were unmemorable, the choreography more or less to match.
The single interesting feature seems to have been the bicycle
with a nervous Serge Lifar continually pumping up the tyres in
the wings instead of practising a few discreet entrechats. *Jack in
the Box* was no better – a variety of dolls hopping out of a
nursery toy box, performing solos and pas de deux and hopping
back again, all to music by Erik Satie and decorated by André
Derain. It was a commonplace affair, though I treasure a
photograph of Shura Danilova in 'black face' as a blackamoor
doll.

The Triumph of Neptune was a very different kettle of fish.
Written for his English audiences, whose faithfulness over the
years had warmed Diaghilev's heart, it was pure English
pantomime of the late nineteenth century. Sacheverell Sitwell,
who wrote the 'book' for this harlequinade, introduced Diaghilev to Mr Pollock of Hoxton and Mr Webb of Old Street –
the last surviving exponents of the nineteenth-century 'penny
plain, tuppence coloured' theatrical prints for children's model
theatres. These were based on drawings by Rowlandson and the
Cruikshank brothers, and were so successful that Pollock's toy
theatres still exist today. Diaghilev was delighted by the
charming scenes and characters and also by the two old men in
their Dickensian shops. He took many prints back to his hotel,
and later they graced the ballet in adaptations made by a close
collaborator, Prince Shervadshidze. The music was composed
by the Englishman Lord Berners, a droll, dilettante figure of
varied artistic talents, and the Lyceum audiences loved it.
There were twelve scenes: a sailor hero, two explorers and a
journalist setting out on a voyage which led to cliff-hanging
adventures involving ogres' caverns, a shipwreck, the Fairy
Queen in her kingdom, Neptune and 'The Villain'. Mr Kirby's
Flying Ballet was recruited for the fairy kingdom – very
effective to watch, and very uncomfortable to do. In *A Midsummer Night's Dream* I, too, have flown with Mr Kirby, whose
harness, pinioning one firmly between the legs, we used to call
Kirby's Grip! *The Triumph of Neptune* ended with a transformation scene to Neptune's kingdom where the sailor becomes a prince and marries the sea-god's daughter.

Within this excellent piece of nonsense was a gem of a solo
for a black servant called Snowball, danced by Balanchine
himself. The critic Cyril Beaumont judged it 'remarkable' and
in his book *The Diaghilev Ballet in London* described it as 'a
dance full of subtly contrasted rhythms, strutting walks,
mincing steps, and surging backward bendings of the body,
borrowed from the cake-walk, the whole invested with a
delicious humour derived from the mood of the dance, a
paradoxical blend of pretended nervous apprehension and
blustering confidence.' I find this fascinating. Here is Balanchine, the great classicist, now revered as the Petipa of the

twentieth century, showing his youthful instinct and talent for everything but classicism. His performances sound vigorous, robust, full of character and humour – all aspects of his own personality. He was lucky that his later world reputation was, in fact, a true one – he *did* become the great classicist, through his own vision and skill.

In this he was unlike Nijinsky, who will always bear a less than just reputation. He became known as the 'God of the Dance', but in reality he was a rather short young man with a badly proportioned body and the heaviest of legs who happened to possess a phenomenal jump, the grace of a woman in movement and matchless facility for the ballet. As a result he danced all the classic rôles at the Maryinsky, then with the Ballets Russes, culminating in his famous *Spectre de la Rose* which the public demanded all over the world. He hated this ballet – hated dancing in it and was infinitely depressed by its continuing success. His greatest talent lay in the instinctive creation of character, rôles which were weird, semi-grotesque, half-human and half-animal. Opportunities came with *Petrushka* and the Golden Slave in *Shéhérazade* – in his own choreography for the Faun in Debussy's *L'Après-midi d'un Faune* and in his last work for the company, on an American tour, Richard Strauss's *Till Eulenspiegel*. Diaghilev never saw this ballet – nor did Europe – but, from still photographs I can see an uncanny interpretation of Strauss's marvellous musical portrait. To me, Nijinsky's tragedy lies far more within his entrapment as a classical virtuoso than in his later madness – and, who knows, the one may have led to the other.

Perhaps I have some understanding of this entrapment through my own theatrical experience. Attempting to move from the ballet into the dramatic theatre, I was immediately cast as Titania and Ondine – it wasn't a disaster but I was quite wrong, and I knew it. When I was able to shake myself free from this ethereal, balletic image to play rôles of real character – Sally Bowles in John Van Druten's *I am a Camera*, Sabina in Thornton Wilder's *Skin of Our Teeth*, and in Restoration comedy – it was a success, bringing a marvellous feeling of release.

After the winter season in London, the Ballets Russes was

back in Monte Carlo for the new year of 1927 and Balanchine
was back to his opera chores again. Verdi's *La Traviata* was
among his first six operas between January and April and he
found it a revealing experience. Bernard Taper quotes him:
'From Verdi's way of dealing with the chorus I learned how to
handle the corps de ballet, the ensemble, the soloists – how to
make the soloists stand out against the corps de ballet and when
to give them time to rest.'

At this time he had a serious accident during a rehearsal,
damaging his knee so badly that even an operation could not
restore it to full strength. He was quite relieved – he could now
give all his concentration to choreography and leave unremit-
ting classwork to others. Though he could not know it, he
would soon be on the brink of his greatest stylistic invention for
the theatre, a ballet which he would rearrange and alter over the
years but one that would always retain its purity and freshness.

8
Apollo

On 30 April 1927, in Monte Carlo, Diaghilev presented another modern experiment, *La Chatte*, with music by Henri Sauguet – which was good – choreography by Balanchine – even better – and designs by the 'Constructivist' Russian brothers, Gabo and Pevsner – best of all. In the many photographs which were taken at the dress rehearsals and during early performances the décor and costumes look amazing, even today. At the time they created a sensation. The stage was hung with shiny black American cloth, the furniture was made from mica and talc in unexpected geometric shapes, the costumes were largely of celluloid, and when the lighting played upon the stage the effect was beautiful and unmistakably 'It'. Diaghilev was visually into the jazz age.

The plot of the ballet was an adaptation of an Aesop fable – a cat is changed into a young woman through the love of a young man. After a blissful interlude she reverts to type and, chasing a mouse, she becomes a cat again to the despair of the young man, whose death she causes. The critic of the *London Sphere* wrote, '*The Cat* is Euclid out of Aesop', because Balanchine had matched his choreography to the geometric and dynamic setting. The more I read about this ballet the more I wish I could have danced in it.

The original Cat was a lovely ballerina called Olga Spessivt-seva. The rôle was written for her, she took part in the dress rehearsal and the photo-call but, according to Alicia Markova,

Spessivtseva sprained her foot at a final rehearsal and a young, lesser dancer, Alice Nikitina, took over – in a matter of hours Balanchine arranged a simpler version of the part for her. Nikitina danced it at the opening in Monte Carlo and later in Paris and London. With the ballet's continuing success Alicia also danced the Cat and, with justifiable pride, she speaks of Balanchine's reinstatement for her of the original virtuoso choreography. He was wonderful in this respect – he could adapt, modify, heighten, even completely rewrite dances for each individual talent. He always wanted each dancer to seem dazzling and irreplaceable, which also served to show his choregoraphy to best advantage. How different from the régime of the English ballet: for us, all choreography was firmly set with the interpretations of the first cast. No matter if one's legs were longer, one's jump higher or lower, one's pirouettes faster or slower, that was *it* – no deviation, even for greater brilliance, was ever allowed. It was a short-sighted and depressing policy.

During the summer of 1927 Balanchine's marriage to Tamara, always a little shaky, finally came to an end. It must have been a difficult situation for her – a woman of great personal ambition, yet with no position of importance in the company – to be constantly in her husband's shadow. She was attractive and flirtatious and had a variety of admirers, but she disliked Monte Carlo and found her life there an irritation and a bore. She found Georges rather a bore too – he was busy and happy, doing the work he liked best, while she wanted change, new interests, new experiences. Also, of course, she must have realized that her talents were minor ones in comparison to his – never an easy situation in a theatrical marriage. Late in life, Balanchine spoke briefly of this time to Solomon Volkov. 'The first time I got married I was young, I didn't care in the least . . . then we both went abroad. And there, you look around, and there are so many marvellous women.' He certainly had self-knowledge. He spoke of something which meant a lot to him: 'My wife, Tamara, began moving away from our life, our *Russian* life', and he talked of the increasing gulf between them as the interests they shared grew further and further apart. So the marriage was bound to end, and it proved a release for them both.

On their parting he gave her a unique present – two solos for her new career with Balieff's then famous Chauve Souris company: *Grotesque Espagnol*, to music by Albeniz, and *Sarcasm*, to a Prokoviev piano solo. She danced them many times with success, and is proud of being the first exponent of Balanchine choreography in America when the Chauve Souris opened a season in New York on 10 October 1927.

She did not remarry – Balanchine, on the other hand almost made an alternative career of marriage. But at this time, with no immediate prospect of divorce from Tamara, he turned to one of his oldest friends from his Imperial School days, Shura Danilo-va – delightful, amusing and Russian to the core. She became Diaghilev's last ballerina, a dancer of great talent and personal-ity, and she and Georges set up house together in Monte Carlo. This happy and theatrically rewarding relationship was to last for four years.

For the remainder of 1927 Balanchine's professional life was divided between the ubiquitous opera ballets, the current vogue for modernity and a few forays into the past. He made a new arrangement of Tchaikovsky's *Swan Lake*, Act II, for Spessiv-tseva and a smaller than usual corps de ballet, to fit the resources of the Ballets Russes. He deleted most of the boring, old-fashioned mime scenes and the Swan Queen and Prince Siegfried danced these passages instead, an adaptation made by the Bolshoi and Kirov companies in Russia also. Would that we could have done the same in London.

I suspect that both Balanchine and Diaghilev were happy to be working again with Tchaikovsky: they loved both the man and his music, for every note spelt out Russia and St Petersburg in the classical tradition which meant so much to them. Diaghilev had tried a great experiment in 1921 in London, a wonderful Léon Bakst production of the complete *Sleeping Princess* – no longer *The Sleeping Beauty* – to avoid confusion with the English pantomime. He wanted it to be his crowning achievement, his homage to the great composer who, strangely, was considered of little account in western Europe at that time. He even presented Petipa's original Princess Aurora, Carlotta

Brianza, by this time very old, in the mime rôle of the wicked
fairy Carabosse. But it was a disaster – the public, expecting
scandalous innovation from Diaghilev, neither liked nor understood a production which seemed reactionary. They persisted
in their contempt for Tchaikovsky's music and the theatre was
half empty; the production was withdrawn, and a despairing
Diaghilev was left with astronomical debts and a broken spirit.
He never fully recovered from this experience.

Nevertheless, the European public in the late twenties was
happy to patronize a single act of an old classic ballet. Balanchine rearranged many of the divertissements in Act III of
Sleeping Beauty, which was given as *Aurora's Wedding*, and
this, with Act II of *Swan Lake*, kept alive the Petipa–
Tchaikovsky tradition until the full *Sleeping Beauty* was given
an English production by the Sadler's Wells Ballet in 1937.

Meanwhile the operas continued – from the well-known *Die
Meistersinger, Un Ballo in Maschera* and *Don Giovanni*, to
one-act operas with amazing titles like *Siòr Todéro Brontolon*
and *La Fille d'Abdoubarahah!* And in the spring of 1928 Anna
Pavlova's company was in Paris at the same time as the Ballets
Russes. She planned a South American tour later that year and
commissioned two dances from Balanchine – *Aleko* to music
by Rachmaninov, and *Polka Grotesque* to music which is now
forgotten; these were danced by Nina Kirsanova and Thadée
Slavinsky. Pavlova also discussed with Balanchine a possible
solo which he would write specifically for her – Scarlatti's
music was suggested – but it came to nothing. What a missed
opportunity: one would love to know the type of choreography
he would have invented to show this unique dancer to best
advantage.

Back in Monte Carlo, Balanchine now began work on his first
great, lasting ballet, now known as *Apollo*. The original title
was *Apollon Musagète*, and the music and slight libretto had
been written by Stravinsky to a commission from Mrs Elizabeth
Sprague Coolidge, a rich American patron of the arts.
Stravinsky's music, spare, rhythmic and a little acid, had
always appealed strongly to Georges: he had attempted to stage
Pulcinella in Russia and had already choreographed *Le Chant
du Rossignol*, but this was to be the first collaboration between

the two men. The cast was small – Apollo, Serge Lifar; Terpsichore, Alice Nikitina; Calliope, Lubov Tchernicheva; Polyhymnia, Felia Doubrovska. There were three further, shadowy figures – Leto, mother of Apollo, and two goddesses – but their appearance was minimal and they did not dance. The setting and costumes were designed by a 'Sunday' painter called André Bauchant and this choice was uncharacteristic of Diaghilev. The décor was acceptable enough, but when Coco Chanel designed new costumes the following year they were much more successful.

Many descriptions have been written of the creation and early rehearsals of this ballet, and one aspect has always surprised me – the number of people watching Balanchine at work, breathing down his neck. Diaghilev; Stravinsky; Boris Kochno; André Derain, the designer; Nicholas Nabokov, the composer; funny little Bauchant who drove everyone mad with his constant chatter – it must have been like a salon. All the choreographers with whom I worked regularly – de Valois, Ashton, Massine, Helpmann – wanted only the cast, a rehearsal pianist and silence. No one else came to the studio or to the stage while we worked and attention was undivided. So here is another example of Balanchine's 'difference'. He must have possessed an extraordinary gift of concentration to be able to ignore all these distractions while engaged in the business of invention, and he may even have been unaware of the audience at his shoulder.

Diaghilev was thrilled with what he saw taking shape before him. It reminded him of the Maryinsky and Petipa, only now it was in the manner of 1928 and with a score by Stravinsky – a mixture which he could appreciate better than anyone else. His favourite, Serge Lifar, was at the centre of the ballet throughout. Not a strong technician, Lifar was fortunate to have Georges as his choreographer, for Balanchine arranged the movements and steps to disguise Lifar's weaknesses and to heighten the beauty of his carriage and fine figure. Indeed, after the immensely successful première many references were made to Lifar's technical virtuosity – as with *La Chatte* – and how there was no choreographic feat which he could not perform. Illusion plays an important part in any ballet: a skilled dancer can make an audience see more grace, line, elevation and brilliance than are actually there, and can create the greatest illusion of all – effortlessness. Pavlova and Nijinsky are supreme examples, but in *Apollo* the art of illusion lay with the choreographer.

This beautiful and simple ballet is still with us today in the repertoire of the New York City Ballet, and I think it will last as long as there are companies to present it. There have been many Apollos and many Muses, and over the years some of Balanchine's alterations to his original choreography have been resented by the public and critics. Change is rarely welcomed and is invariably found to be less appealing than the original conception, even when that conception has been found wanting.

Critics are a strange breed. They come in many forms: there are those who know something of the art they criticize, and those who do not; those who love the theatre, and those who patently do not; those who write for their own self-glorification, and those who are soured by their own lack of creative or interpretative talent; and – to me, worst of all – those who bring their own prejudices to bear on everything they see and hear. Ballet criticism can be excessively flowery – adjectives cascade over the paper and prose becomes precious. A highly regarded American critic, Edwin Denby, wrote these words after his first exposure to *Apollo*:

> Extraordinary is the richness with which he [Balanchine] can, with only four dancers, create a sustained and more and more satisfying impression of the grandness of man's creative genius, depicting it concretely in its grace, its sweet wit, its force and boldness, and with the constant warmth of its sensuous complicity with physical beauty. *Apollo* is an homage to the academic tradition – and the first work in the contemporary classic style, but it is an homage to classicism's sensuous loveliness as well as to its brilliant exactitude and its science of dance effect . . . and it leaves at the end, despite its innumerable incidental inventions, a sense of bold, open, effortless and limpid grandeur.

London has an excellently ribald satirical magazine, *Private Eye*, which contains a section of maximum pleasure called 'Pseud's Corner' – pompous, idiotic writing from all sources contributed by wickedly watchful readers. Denby is my candidate for this column; I find his review a perfect example of Grade I 'pseudery'. In itself this doesn't matter – it is unimportant – but there is something else here which I do mind very much.

Ballet as an art has always been beset by the 'arty' balletomane, the would-be esoteric. In my day, the 1940s and '50s, they were mainly women of indeterminate age who haunted every auditorium, dressed like Pavlova for *Tzigane*, talking loudly of the finer points of choreography and technique about which they clearly knew nothing. The concert hall and the art gallery also suffer from their own built-in bores, but I think that, on the whole, they are more educated and more adult. When critics indulge in the same kind of rubbish in their reviews, I believe real damage is done to the only people who matter – the general public. They become confused; they imagine that because they have simply enjoyed a performance and have remembered it later with pleasure that this is somehow wrong – that they have missed the vital element.

All dancers must have heard the phrase, as I have a hundred times, 'Yes, I love the ballet but of course I don't understand it – I wish I did.' Then one tries – struggles – to make people see that there is in fact nothing to *understand*. If there was, we would all have failed miserably. Surprise and pleasure in the movements and patterns performed on the stage are the only things that matter; the technique, and the way it is achieved, are of importance only to the performer. Too many people read of entrechats, pirouettes and arabesques and feel they should be able to identify every one. Why? What possible added pleasure can this bring? When I look at a picture by Rembrandt, I have no wish to know how he achieved his miraculous chiaroscuro – it would seem irrelevant to all that he wanted to convey in his finished work.

Balanchine hated pseudery; so did Stravinsky, who made a tired, amused comment after a particularly fulsome 'reading' of the hidden meanings in a piece of his music – 'In the end I almost believed it myself!' It is of course all too easy to criticize – I am doing it now, myself, but I think with reason. What few critics can ever do is to demonstrate how something that they have damned might be improved; so, for what it's worth, here is my translation of Edwin Denby:

> Balanchine, with only four dancers on an almost bare stage, has created a ballet which is beautiful, simple and grand. Perfectly matching Stravinsky's contemporary score, this is nevertheless, true classic dancing in the Petipa tradition. Balanchine has the great gift of blending the old and the new in invention of originality and beauty. There are no tricks – the choreography is simple and stylish and the final effect might well please both Mozart and David Hockney, Stockhausen and Michelangelo.

I am not a critic, but is this not more clear, more digestible and more understandable to the general public? It would certainly be more acceptable to choreographer and dancers, but – I am biased!

After the première of *Apollo* at the Théâtre Sarah Bernhardt on 12 June, the Paris critics were enthusiastic. The *Times* Paris correspondent wrote:

> M. Lifar is the Etruscan Apollo of Veii come to life. . .He maintains the lines and gestures of archaic sculpture. Compared with the god, the Muses . . . seem strangely 19th century in their formal ballet skirts and tight mauve bodices [the Bauchant costumes], but the contrast is not unpleasant, and Mmes Nikitina, Tchernicheva, and Doubrovska convey with their accustomed grace and beauty the special attributes of each.

The ballet was then shown in London, where the *Times* critic took a more jaundiced view, concentrating on the music:

> It used to be said that the Russian Ballet would not be much without Stravinsky; his latest production makes us fear that soon it will not be much with him. . .the work was applauded doggedly by a large audience, whose faithfulness was to be rewarded later with the popular *Firebird* . . . *Apollo Musagète* is a very solemn matter. It is not meant to please, like *Cimarosiana*, or to be exciting, like the *Firebird*. It succeeds in avoiding both pitfalls. The music is not even ugly, merely a listless meandering of commonplaces, thickly scored for strings. No percussion, no strident harmonies, no 'Zip'!

Francis Toye, writing in *The Morning Post*, began with the choreography, which he found:

> extremely ingenious and beautiful at times, particularly as regards some of the held poses, but the whole is too tenuous to hold the attention so long. As for the music, Stravinsky seems to have copied another famous composer in searching for progress in the antique, for the influence of Bach and some of the early Italians is strong ... Further acquaintance will show to what extent the composer has concealed his own personality underneath this rather obvious surface. Lifar as Apollo and Nikitina as Terpischore had most of the work to do, and did it notably better than their colleagues.

Finally Richard Capell, who had seen every Diaghilev season since the Paris première in 1909, based his *Daily Mail* review on a comment overheard on the first night, that *Apollo* was 'Quite too strorrd'nary for words!' He continued:

> The strorrd'nariness of the new *Apollo* lay in no luxury but in the singular austerity of the exercises on Parnassus' top. But first we have a prelude, and the birth of Apollo. He issues – a pretty fancy – from a large hand-painted valentine, signed Bauchant. Apollo, whom goddesses unwrap from his swaddling clothes, is a strikingly fit, athletic stripling – none other, of course, than Serge Lifar. He has need of his intensive training, for the choreography [by Balanchine] which he has to undertake looks incredibly difficult. The first curtain goes down on a pose in swimming attitude, Apollo being supported on his stomach by the soles of the goddesses' feet.

Of the Muses he wrote: 'Apollo, maintaining the impassiveness of an idol, puts the three through paces which no doubt symbolise the cruel arduousness of the artistic callings ... The end is Apollo's apotheosis. Lifar deserved it.'

It is always interesting looking back over old reviews, especially for performers. Although the excerpts above are taken from undeniably 'poor' reviews, there is a humour in the writing which today's criticism often lacks. And it is kindly humour, quite without malice; this is refreshing, even when one is in complete disagreement with the writer's views. Only a single omission on the part of the three gentlemen quoted seems to me 'too strorrd'nary' – not one of them, however much he disliked the ballet, noticed the birth of an unmistakable, twentieth-century, classical style. Yet in *Design for the Ballet*, which was published in 1978, Mary Clarke and Clement Crisp have written: 'It is only in 1928 when Balanchine was entrusted with Stravinsky's *Apollo* that the return of choreography to some form of pre-eminence is evident.' Hindsight is always interesting.

Robert Helpmann told me years ago, 'Don't keep your own reviews, keep other people's.' We were at the Edinburgh Festival in 1954 before touring America with the Old Vic *Midsummer Night's Dream*, and our Bottom was a dear comic actor from Yorkshire, Stanley Holloway. Every critic compared him unfavourably with Ralph Richardson in 1937, whom they said had been 'incomparable'. With glee, Helpmann – who had been in the same production – fished out the old press notices, and there we read how glum, inaudible and generally boring Sir Ralph had been deemed at that time! It is a comforting story.

The production of *Apollo* caused the only rupture between Balanchine and Diaghilev during these years, the impresario behaving in a very petty and malicious way. Money was at the root of the trouble. Alice Nikitina was the protégée of the then Lord Rothermere: he was partly supporting the Ballets Russes, and consequently she was the dancer chosen to replace Spessivtseva in *La Chatte* and then given the rôle of Terpsichore. Balanchine wrote a lovely solo for her in *Apollo*, but after the first performances in Paris, Diaghilev ordered the solo to be cut – he had decided that it bored him. Georges, who had wanted Danilova for the rôle, was furious and told Diaghilev bluntly that it wasn't the solo which bored but the dancer. During the impasse which followed word was received that Lord Rothermere had withdrawn his patronage. His decision seems to have been quite unconnected with any internal difficulties within the company, but poor Nikitina became the whipping boy: Diaghilev turned on her and treated her cruelly and humiliatingly in front of the full company. Eventually the solo was reinstated after a face-saving delay by Diaghilev; he

then had to concede further, allowing Danilova to share the part
– which, of course, she danced beautifully, making it more and
more her own.

A few months later Serge Grigoriev, the régisseur of the
company, talked with Diaghilev about the renewal of certain
contracts, Balanchine's among them. Diaghilev lost his
temper – Sacheverell Sitwell says that his voice rose to a high
falsetto at such moments – and ranted against his choreographer, shouting that he had no wish to renew his contract.
Grigoriev wisely waited for a quieter moment, when the impresario said to him with studied indifference, 'Do as you like',
whereupon Grigoriev rushed to secure Balanchine's signature
before there could be further dispute.

There is no record of Balanchine having any knowledge of
this fracas. In any case his thoughts were always on his work,
particularly at the time of *Apollo*, which he later described as
'the turning point in my life'. Stravinsky's music was the key,
forcing him to pare his choreography to a minimum and thus
discover his own true style. As he put it himself, it made him
'dare to not use all my ideas' – ungrammatical, revealing and
impressive. Timing in life is all, and it was the greatest good
fortune, for these two gifted men as much as for their public,
that they met and began a unique partnership under the wing of
Sergey Diaghilev. Though Balanchine would always defer to
Stravinsky, saying, rightly, that the rhythmic pattern of the
music came first and the translation of these rhythms into
vision was secondary, Stravinsky felt a similar debt to the
choreographer. His music had been used many times in the
theatre, but he had never been happy with the result. Now, at
last, he had found a matching spirit; he wrote later that *Apollo*,
'with its groups, movements and lines of great dignity and
plastic elegance as inspired by the beauty of classical forms',
was the ideal complement to his score. The two men became
great friends; it was a friendship which would last all their lives
and prove perennially fruitful.

Debate will always rage about the influence of Stravinsky's
music on Balanchine's subsequent career. Without it would he
have written so many 'abstracts' at the expense of the 'story'
ballet? Would he have become, as some people think, so 'arid'?

There are many views: Ninette de Valois finds abstract ballets 'a bore'; Frederick Ashton likes a few but thinks they 'lack emotion', that 'everything is held in'; Alicia Markova says simply that he was 'a wonderful choreographer'. And critics all over the world veer this way and that, depending on their personal taste and preference. I love Balanchine's 'abstractions', though I agree that they lack drama and emotion; of course they do – they must, by their very nature. But in place of this there is a cleanness, a clarity of line and movement, a musicality and, above all, fantastic invention.

I have never ceased to be amazed by the changes that this man could ring from the limited repertoire of classical steps. He created hundreds of dances with no hint of repetition, and possessed a masterly command of geometric pattern with the corps de ballet flowing to and fro in extraordinary complexity and yet simplicity. No one would want a diet of this alone – nor of relentless *Petrushkas* and *Polovtsian Dances*. But a balance between the two is surely ideal. Balanchine's gift of invention makes me think of the endless permutations of the human face: two eyes, two ears, a nose and a mouth – and yet, however long one lives, when does one ever see exactly the same face twice? The variety in the measured arrangement of these features is infinite – his choreography has the same quality.

9
Prodigal Son

The year 1929 was to be the last of Diaghilev's life and the end of his Ballets Russes. The career of every member of his company was about to change drastically, but each would carry to the grave the unique influence of the great impresario. For a choreographer this was even greater than for a dancer, and Balanchine still had two ballets of importance to compose after the exceptional *Apollo*.

The first was a relatively small work of quiet charm and style, *The Gods Go A-Begging*, which was premièred with success on 16 July 1928 at His Majesty's Theatre in London. The music, by Handel, had been arranged by the celebrated and waspish Thomas Beecham, who also conducted the London performances, even though he is on record as loathing dancers slightly more than singers! Diaghilev's finances must have been at a low ebb as the décor used was the Bakst *Daphnis and Chloë*, Fokine's 1912 ballet; the costumes came from Nijinska's 1924 *Tentations de la Bergère*, designed by Juan Gris – and they had originally been designed for an even earlier ballet. Though this sounds like a hotch-potch, the result was elegant and delightful. Boris Kochno had supplied a mild 'book' about noble ladies and gentlemen at a *fête champêtre*, and a shepherd and a serving maid who, in a dénouement, reveal themselves as god and goddess. For Danilova, Balanchine created a rôle of immense charm; his inspiration was the painter Watteau, and the resulting ballet – though quite unlike *Apollo* in every respect – showed the continuing development of his own style. Ninette de Valois also choreographed *The Gods Go A-Begging* to the same lovely music some years later, and it was the first leading rôle I danced after only three weeks with her company in 1942.

In Monte Carlo in early 1929 Balanchine tackled six further opera ballets before starting work on his last production for Diaghilev – Prokoviev's *Prodigal Son*. He also made his first foray into a new field, one that he would later come to know well – musical revue. Charles B. Cochran was a noted British impresario of his day, specializing in sophisticated shows for intelligent people and not, in his words, 'for the tired business man'. He invited Georges to London to choreograph a sequence for his 1929 revue, *Wake Up and Dream*, with music and lyrics by Cole Porter and a cast which included a Viennese dancer and mime artist, Tilly Losch. The particular number was 'What Is This Thing Called Love?', perhaps an apt title for Balanchine at this time. Today Shura Danilova, speaking of her relationship with him, feels that the life of stress and upheaval in Russia from which they had suffered had taken its toll, especially in his case. In a wistful phrase she says, 'Perhaps he had not yet learned how to love another human being', and indeed this does seem true.

The choreography for *Wake Up and Dream* must represent one of the rare occasions when Balanchine received no credit on the programme – it was given to Tilly Losch. I doubt if this caused him any discomfort; it was a small chore he had performed, but a valuable one for him. Now, back in Monte Carlo, his mind was fully occupied with ideas for the Prokoviev ballet. But first he wrote another quick, 'modish' work, *Le Bal*, to a score by Vittorio Rieti commissioned by Diaghilev. In spite of scenery and costumes by Giorgio de Chirico, Danilova in the central rôle and Georges himself in a Spanish pas de trois, it was unmemorable – a rather tricky piece by all accounts. Agnes de Mille, the American choreographer, saw it and also the bicycling *Pastorale* and cared for neither. She particularly disliked the use of revue and variety jokes: she cites the old one of two people advancing towards each other at top speed with hands outstretched, missing each other and continuing into the wings, which she found both trivial and tedious. She is not over-enthusiastic about *La Chatte* either, but has nothing but praise for *Prodigal Son*.

Like all good productions it suffered from upheavals and problems throughout the rehearsal period. The first stumbling block was the painter commissioned to design the sets and costumes, Georges Rouault – a little, shabby man who sat at rehearsals watching intently and mutely until one day he sprang into action to show how he could balance a chair on his nose! A painfully slow worker, he repeatedly refused to let Diaghilev see the designs he was planning. Eventually Diaghilev lost patience, got hold of the key to his room when he knew Rouault was out, found hundreds of sketches lying all over the floor, and without hesitation stole as many as he could carry away. From these the ubiquitous Prince Shervadshidze created the unmistakable Rouault décor, and Vera Soudeikina – later Vera Stravinsky – made the finished designs for the equally effective costumes.

Boris Kochno's libretto was based on a short story by Pushkin, *The Stationmaster*, with its description of a little Russian station house hung with engravings of the biblical story. As a result the ballet became a very Russian interpretation of the Prodigal's youth, which added a mysterious, Slav element to the drama of the original. Diaghilev had only once before presented anything taken from the Bible – *La Légende de Joseph* – and he was a little uneasy about the outcome, particularly about Georges and his ability to cope with an emotional theme. He seems to have thought of his choreographer as purely 'intellectual' in his approach, which is surely strange after *Barabau*, *The Triumph of Neptune*, *The Gods Go A-Begging* and the romantic Tchaikovsky arrangements – let alone his wild personal clowning and gift for characterization.

The finished work amazed everyone. It was not only highly dramatic and emotional but contained scenes of horrifying decadence, as well as one of tenderness and fatherly love at the close which left much of the audience in tears. Balanchine loved working on this ballet: the tall Felia Doubrovska was his Siren and he experimented on her, choreographing previously unheard of acrobatic movement. Before the first night she became nervous of the eroticism and suggestiveness of her rôle, but Balanchine's conception was right and she had a tremendous success. He also gave Lifar another great part as the Prodigal, saying late in life that no subsequent Prodigal had ever matched him. Agnes de Mille has great admiration for Edward Villella's portrayal and I found Baryshnikov – in the only performance I have seen – magical.

As so often in the theatre, some of the most vivid touches came almost as afterthoughts. At the final rehearsal Balanchine ordered completely bald heads for the twelve drinking companions of the Prodigal – the effect of this, combined with their evilly scuttling bodies, was frightening and disgusting. And, for the Promenade when the Siren and 'friends' leave with the spoils stripped from the Prodigal, he discovered some final extra bars of music. He at once used these imaginatively by turning the long drinking table upside down to represent a boat, placing the men inside – some rowing, some in the stern with long trumpets – and with the Siren arched at the prow, her long, blood-red cloak pulled out and up as a sail. This was accomplished at the last minute – Balanchine meant to change the end of the scene before the second performance, but he liked the effect so much that it is still with us today.

In the midst of this satisfying creativity one sour note sounded – the composer. Prokoviev must have been a difficult man at the best of times but the production of this ballet found him at his worst. He had arrived with firm, pre-conceived ideas about the style of choreography for his music and fully expected an excess of naturalism, which would nevertheless include a Siren both delicate and wistful. He loathed what he saw and said so forcibly, but fortunately Diaghilev paid not the slightest attention. He did not cross swords with Balanchine at this point, but there was a nasty moment to come.

Composers and librettists received royalties, but choreographers did not, for the ridiculous reason that their work could not be seen on paper. Stravinsky, though notably mean with money, had given Georges a sixth of his own royalties after *Apollo* – heaven-sent for an impoverished member of the Ballets Russes – and, with the successful addition of *Prodigal Son* to the repertoire, Georges made the singular mistake of asking Prokoviev if he would do the same. Describing this moment to Bernard Taper, Balanchine said, 'Prokoviev shouted at me, "Why should you get money? Who are you? You're nothing but a lousy balletmaster. Get out!" ' And he did. It was the last time he ever used Prokoviev's music for a ballet.

There was only one other occasion when a composer was unpleasant to him – Rachmaninov, after a London concert. With Danilova, Georges had clawed his way through a long queue to be present: they were overwhelmed by Rachmaninov's playing and afterwards joined another queue of admirers waiting to pay their tribute. The composer stood in a corner of the green room – tall, with a glum expression on his long, lugubrious face. (I always thought he looked like a sad old horse). Eventually it was their turn and, as Balanchine told Solomon Volkov:

> We bowed – 'How do you do? – it was so wonderful . . . this is Danilova from the Maryinsky and I'm Balanchivadze. We're dancers from the Maryinsky Theatre – we're ecstatic – we always come to your concerts – you're a great pianist'. Rachmaninov was silent. I went on humbly, 'If you would allow, I would like to ask you respectfully . . .' Rachmaninov interrupted me rudely – 'What'? – I tried to continue – 'Your marvellous *Elegy* . . . perhaps you would permit me to do something with your music – for dancing . . .' Rachmaninov began shouting, 'Have you lost your mind' You're crazy! Dance to my music? How dare you! Get out! Get out!'

Since then the *Paganini Variations* have proved an inspiration for several choreographers, but not for Balanchine.

Prodigal Son was premièred in Paris at the Théâtre Sarah Bernhardt with the unyielding composer as conductor. The ballet was then seen in London, with great success, during the summer season at the Royal Opera House, Covent Garden. In the main it was a critical as well as a public success, though the London *Times* again showed some discrepancy between the views of its resident critic and those of its Paris correspondent. In London Rouault's colours were 'glowing . . . caught up in the velvets of the costumes', while in Paris, the same paper said, 'the muddy colours which this painter affects are entirely unsuitable to stage decoration' . . . though the writer later admitted that 'the grouping of the guests in green and white around M. Lifar in brilliant blue is extremely effective'. (How can green, white and brilliant blue be 'muddy'?) This seems a perfect example of how differently two pairs of eyes can interpret the same sight – demonstrating yet again that theatre criticism is so often a matter of personal taste and preference, and not of authority.

After the final performance on 26 July, Diaghilev summoned the company to the stage to say goodbye until the autumn. He made a charming speech, telling them of the busy year ahead with its full programme of engagements, hoping they would rest well during the summer break and thanking everyone 'for the excellent work you have done, which has been largely responsible for any success we may have had'. He moved slowly among the dancers, shaking hands with each and leaving around them the scent of his almond blossom hair pomade. He was already very ill. His appearance was alarming – ashen, puffy with feverish eyes – but the company was not worried, for there had been similar moments and yet his constitution seemed indestructible. An old friend of mine, Edward Gordon Craig, said of Diaghilev, 'He could look the oldest man in the town when you met him at noon and, at eight, when the curtain was about to go up, he would look the youngest.' So it had always been and, as the company left for a single performance at Ostend and on to Vichy for a final week, Diaghilev went to Paris and then travelled slowly, via his beloved galleries and museums, to his final destination – Venice.

The week in Vichy was immensely successful: many devotees of the company had travelled long distances to see the performances, and the many curtain calls were fortified by a particularly resounding basso 'Bravo'. There was no *Prodigal Son* or *Apollon Musagète* on the last night: it was a moment for old favourites, all by Massine – *Cimarosiana*, *Le Tricorne* and *La Boutique Fantasque*, with Georges (this time without the green whiskers) in the Mazurka. The 'Bravos' came from the throat of Fyodor Chaliapin, who had been present for the whole engagement. The great bass was as gigantic off stage as any Boris Godunov or Mephistopheles. Of immense height and presence,

he affected everyone he touched – particularly women, who fell
to him as the 'mille tre' Don Giovanni. His charm was legendary; Shura Danilova spoke of it as the greatest she ever encoun-
tered and added, 'He was full of naughtiness – one night he
would be on his knees with the aristocrats, weeping and singing
"God save the Tsar", and the next night with the Revolutionaries, equally moved and singing their song from the heart.' Still
speaking of charm, she said firmly, 'Georges had *no* charm' – an
astonishing statement and the only time I have ever heard this
opinion expressed.

From Vichy Balanchine went to London where he had an
engagement to choreograph and dance in the first English
talking picture, *Dark Red Roses*. Made by Era Films at the old
Isleworth Studios and directed by Sinclair Hill, it starred the
Canadian actress, Frances Doble, sister-in-law of Sacheverell
Sitwell. It was a typical romantic melodrama of the time –
suspicious sculptor husband, possible intrigue of wife with
likely musician, and so on – and Balanchine's task was to
invent a Claudius–Gertrude 'play within a play' for performance before this trio. He chose music from Mussorgsky's opera
Khovanshchina, portraying the Tartar husband himself, with
Lydia Lopokova and Anton Dolin as wife and lover. It was an
extremely fierce and oriental piece – Lopokova being dragged
around by her hair and Balanchine lopping off Dolin's hands
with an ugly sabre. This, the only Balanchine performance that
I have seen, has all the comic element of a very early film but
with force and bravura shining through unmistakably.

During this time he stayed in Sussex with Lopokova and her
husband, John Maynard Keynes. He had fallen under Lydia's
spell in the early Diaghilev days and was very fond of her; now
he found that her intellectual husband was also quite a wag and
full of high spirits – he is reputed to have danced the can-can at
Bloomsbury parties! They spent many agreeable weeks
together, Keynes insistent on talking about the ballet and
Balanchine equally insistent on talking about economics. And
Georges liked England – he always enjoyed being in or near
London.

On the day of the filming of their sequence, 19 August 1929,
Lydia, Georges and Dolin were ready, in costume, at the studios

in the late afternoon. Georges was in typical, prankish mood and caused poor Lopokova much linguistic confusion. She had been given one line of English dialogue to say to the sculptor before the dance number: 'I wish I could do as well with my feet as you with your hands.' She was very fussed about this, going over and over the line in case she made a mistake. To tease her was irresistible and Balanchine – and indeed Dolin too – offered alternatives, such as 'I wish I could do with my toes as well as you with your nose', with variations, as Balanchine told Bernard Taper many years later.

Time passed and they sat there; apparently nothing was happening. A newspaper boy came into the studio with the late evening papers and Dolin went over to buy one. As he walked back he glanced at the front page, stopped, then shouted, 'Serge Pavlovich est mort.' They couldn't believe it – but there was the little paragraph before them. It stated simply that Diaghilev had died in Venice, from diabetes, in the early hours of the morning. They sat quietly for several hours, Lydia frequently in tears, until they danced for the camera at two o'clock in the morning of the next day.

It had been a difficult death. Venice was like an oven in the summer of 1929 and Diaghilev had lain in a state of high fever for three days. Lifar was there, Kochno was there, Misia Sert and Coco Chanel hovered, but he was unaware of them. When it was all over it was discovered that this great man of the theatre, this 'grand seigneur', possessed one suit, one coat, one hat, one pair of shoes and two badly frayed and almost buttonless shirts. In a memoir written in 1953 Igor Stravinsky said that, when he had money, Diaghilev was generous to a fault – that he was entirely without personal ambition and that everything he achieved was in the cause of art itself. Nearing his own death in America, Stravinsky paid his greatest tribute when he asked to be buried on San Michele, the Venetian island cemetery, beside Sergey Pavlovich, his first patron in St Petersburg when he was a stripling nonentity. And there he lies today.

10
Limbo

With Diaghilev's death the Ballets Russes ceased to exist, crushed by massive debt as much as by lack of leadership. Georges was only one of many left stranded at a time when the future had seemed so secure, and, added to their sorrow at losing their irreplaceable mentor, there was now the worry of finding work. The company scattered – many staying in Europe, some in England, one or two travelling to America – but, in the easy, gipsy way of dancers' lives, their paths continuing to cross in one country or another for many years. Several Diaghilev dancers would work with Balanchine to the end of his and their days.

He was now twenty-five years old, and in the theatre his name and talent had made more than a passing mark. Soon he received an offer from Jacques Rouché, director of the Paris Opéra, to stage Beethoven's two-act ballet, *Les Créatures de Prométhée*. The Opéra ballet company had been in the doldrums for many years – to Rouché's dismay it had become almost a laughing stock with Parisian audiences, and he saw Balanchine as the antidote. So much faith did he have in the young choreographer that he also invited him to become resident *maître de ballet* whenever it might suit him to take up the post.

Prométhée was one thing, but to become the Opéra ballet master was quite another, and Balanchine had no wish to tie himself down so completely at this stage of his career. He was

well aware of the other side of such a post – the internal
politics, the intrigue and back-biting – but, as no decision was
required immediately, he agreed to choreograph the Beethoven
and started rehearsals. But his luck was running out. Two
weeks later he lay seriously ill with pneumonia and the doctors
doubted that he would live through it. Treatment in 1929 was
still surprisingly primitive; he endured the old-fashioned 'cup-
ping' method, after which a slow recovery seemed to begin,
only to give way to pleurisy. For several days he was too ill to
see anyone – as he gradually improved he was visited by one of
Rouché's assistants from the Opéra. What of his future? Could
he continue with the Beethoven ballet?

With the best will in the world he knew that it would be
impossible, and he suggested that Serge Lifar, his leading male
dancer, might continue the choreography. Lifar had arranged
one ballet for Diaghilev, the not very successful *Le Renard*,
which Rouché unfortunately remembered. But Georges assured
him that he could guide Lifar from his convalescent bed, and so
it was agreed. Lifar would have sole credit as choreographer on
the programme, while Georges would keep the fee of ten
thousand francs contracted with Rouché.

During the next seven days Balanchine's bedroom resembled
a Feydeau farce. Doors flew open and banged shut as distraught
people darted in and out – designers, the wardrobe mistress,
dancers, musicians and, perpetually, an uncharacteristically
nervous Lifar. He bombarded Georges with questions about
every single movement, while the invalid became more and
more exhausted. Finally his infuriated doctor took one look at
his patient and told him that pleurisy had given way to
tuberculosis. Immediately all visitors were banned and arrangements were made with a sanatorium in Southern France. But,
for Lifar, all was well – he had got everything he needed from
Georges and waved him away with equanimity.

The pinewoods of the Haute Savoie, near Mont Blanc, are of
great beauty. Mountain ranges and valleys pile one on another;
little wooden houses and farms are dotted everywhere in the
brilliant green; there is the scent of a thousand wild flowers and
the hollow, Tibetan sound of goat and cow bells in the fresh,
clean air. It was the ideal setting for the many sanatoriums of

the twenties and thirties when tuberculosis was still such a scourge.

Balanchine was taken to one of the hospitals at the beginning of November 1929. The snows came and it was icily cold, but it is the crisp, sunny cold of the Alps which has always been considered so healing to the chest and lungs.

He was very ill on arrival – for many weeks he had a high fever which left him weak and helpless. Day after day he lay on the verandah, wrapped to the neck in blankets, in the open air but never in direct sunshine. No visitors came: the hours passed in a strange dream-like awareness when his thoughts became confused and his powers of concentration slipped away. He couldn't read, he couldn't write, and there was no music for him to hear. He was alive but in a state of limbo. In mid-December his temperature gradually became steadier and his strength began to return. But his thoughts continued to elude him and, though he was now more than ever aware of his vocation, not a single idea came to him for a dance, a ballet or a theatre production. Creatively, his mind remained a blank, though he could now concentrate more easily on the progress of his recovery. He was able to give a firm refusal when the sanatorium doctor proposed a major thorax operation; he had lost all faith in surgery since the disastrous treatment of his knee injury.

His recovery continued and the day came when he threw off his blankets and stood steadily on his feet. At first he pottered quietly in the hospital grounds, but soon he was able to take increasingly long walks in the surrounding woods. Indeed his condition improved so rapidly that, early in the New Year, the doctors agreed to release him. They knew, as he did, that his lungs were permanently damaged, but medically there was little more that could be done. What is astonishing – in view of the volume of work he would achieve – is that, later that same year, his left lung collapsed. For the rest of his life it caused him intermittent fever and distress, but he learned to cope with it so well that few people guessed his disability.

On leaving the Haute Savoie Georges travelled to Paris. He felt strangely disoriented during these first days out in the world again and, wanting security, he remembered Rouché's

offer to become the Opéra *maître de ballet*. It seemed much
more attractive now that his own situation was so changed, and
he lost no time in contacting the theatre. Lifar was there to greet
him – full of the success of *Prométhée* in December and of his
own personal triumph. As they talked it became clear that, for
Lifar, Balanchine's presence in the theatre was not exactly a
cause for unbounded joy, and he hinted at many insoluble
difficulties connected with Georges and his possible acceptance
as ballet master. It was typical 'Lifaresquiana' and one might
have expected Balanchine to smell a rat and make an immediate appointment with Jacques Rouché. But, surprisingly, he
accepted Lifar's arguments and left. Perhaps he was again
beginning to doubt his enthusiasm for the post; perhaps his
fatalism rebelled against the exhausting prospect of probable
battles and intrigues. Whatever the reason, he made no effort to
contact Rouché and read in a newspaper soon afterwards that
the Opéra directors had appointed their *new maître de ballet* –
M. Serge Lifar!

By good luck an old friend from the Ballets Russes was also in
Paris. Vera Nemchinova, who had been one of Diaghilev's last
ballerinas, had formed a tiny company which was then dancing
at the Théâtre des Champs Elysées. Balanchine had partnered
her many times, and they had made an elegant and stylish
Prince and Princess in *Aurora's Wedding*. She invited Georges
to choreograph a ballet for her: the theme was the myth of Diana
and Actaeon, the music – for eighteen instruments and piano –
was by Francis Poulenc. Balanchine had lost none of his inner
energy and speed of invention, and *Aubade* was premièred on
21 January with the composer at the piano. Nemchinova's
kindness and good sense had given the still frail choreographer
the fillip he needed, and in the process she had gained a
charming 'vignette' ballet.

Meanwhile, in London, Charles Cochran's sharp eyes and
ears had not missed Balanchine's return to the lists and he
offered him a substantial contract for his new 1930 Revue at the
Pavilion Theatre. The timing could not have been better, and
without a moment's hesitation Georges arrived in London to
start work. And there, waiting to work with him, were Alice
Nikitina, Efimov and – yes – the new Paris Opéra *maître de*

ballet designate, M. Serge Lifar! He was all smiles, kisses and grandiloquent gestures – delightfully transparent, just as if nothing had happened – and Georges, with his easy, equable temperament, had no difficulty in working in perfect harmony and giving Lifar, as always, choreography which would show him to best advantage.

The music and book for the Revue were by Vivian Ellis and Beverley Nichols, but for the dance sequences there were scores by Lord Berners (*Triumph of Neptune*) and Henri Sauguet (*La Chatte*), both old friends. Boris Kochno was engaged for the ballet libretti, and soon this little group was swelled by the addition of several Diaghilev dancers from the old company, notably Constantine Tcherkas. This is one of the greatest pleasures for theatre people – the continual criss-crossing of lives which have shared past experience, whether good or bad. Balanchine must have felt at home in this milieu, at ease with the cast and absorbed in the varied ballets he had undertaken. Cochran had a touch of Diaghilev's flair in the staging of his shows and in his imaginative use of talent. André Derain and Christian Bérard had designed earlier revues, and in 1930 Christopher Wood, Oliver Messel and Rex Whistler all contributed settings and costumes.

The stage of the London Pavilion was far too small for free, full-blooded dancing, so Balanchine's ingenuity was seen to excellent advantage. One of the ballets, much admired by Cecil Beaton, was *Luna Park*, which had a cast of fairground freaks: a Three-headed Man; a Three-legged Man; Nikitina as a One-legged Woman and Lifar as a Six-armed Man, each in their booths. It was intriguing and not a little peculiar but, as Beaton wrote, 'in its peculiar way, beautiful'. There were also pas de deux and solos and several production numbers involving Mr Cochran's Young Ladies and Young Gentlemen – one, called *Tennis*, with Efimov as the Referee among *all* the Young Ladies. Most ingenious was a number called *In a Venetian Theatre*, ostensibly a dance sequence but without a single dance step. Looking at the stage, the audience saw a mirror image of themselves – young women seated in tiered rows watching a play. Everything was conveyed by their, heads, arms and hands as they talked and laughed together, greeted friends, were alarmed, wept and applauded. It was beautifully arranged and performed and, for many people, the hit of the show.

For the first time in his life Balanchine was being paid well and he enjoyed the experience. Neither prudent nor thrifty by nature, he looked on money as a delightful commodity to be spent when one had it, and of little importance when one hadn't. He had left Russia with hardly more than the clothes on his back, so the lure of possessions had never troubled him, but now, with luxuries within reach, he discovered how extremely pleasant they could be. He was looking forward to becoming London's best-dressed man when an invitation from the Royal Danish Ballet took him once more to Europe. He accepted the post of guest ballet master at the Royal Theatre, Copenhagen, for the next five months – a hasty and unwise decision which he, and the Danes, would come to regret.

His assignment was to stage for the company six of Diaghilev's ballets – four by Fokine and two by Massine. It was an extraordinary task for him to undertake. Balanchine did not enjoy the exact re-creation of his own ballets, let alone other people's, and was, in fact, incapable of doing so. He started with Massine's *Le Tricorne* and it emerged with Balanchine choreography – so did Fokine's *Shéhérazade*; *La Boutique Fantasque*, the *Polovtsian Dances*, *Le Spectre de la Rose* and *La Légende de Joseph* were performed by the meticulous Danes in versions which would have produced hysteria from Fokine and black amazement from Massine.

Le Spectre de la Rose was only given once, at a charity performance on 14 December, when Karsavina's role was danced by Ulla Poulsen and Balanchine himself replaced Nijinsky. This decision by Balanchine seems unbelievable – the most famous male rôle in the classical-romantic tradition danced by a character dancer with one lung and a damaged knee! For once in his life Balanchine's excellent judgement had deserted him. Copenhagen would never be a happy city for him, and when his contract was completed in January 1931 relief was felt on both sides. Later a Danish ballet historian would write, 'He [Balanchine] did not make the impression his ability had promised.'

Perhaps his thoughts at this time were too centred on the

Balanchine's father, Meliton
(Ballet Society, Inc.)

Balanchine's mother, Maria
(Ballet Society, Inc.)

Gyorgy and his brother Andrey
(Ballet Society, Inc.)

Balanchine with Tamara Geva in *Etude*, 1923 *(Ballet Society, Inc.)*

Stravinsky (*left*), Madame Kvochinsky, Diaghilev (*center*) and Bakst
(*Bibliothèque de l'Opéra*)

Diaghilev
(Bibliothèque de l'Opéra)

Stravinsky
(Bibliothèque de l'Opéra)

Balanchine in Venice, 1926 *(New York Public Library)*

Alexandra Danilova in
The Gods Go A-Begging, 1928
(Ballet Society, Inc.)

Serge Lifar in
Luna Park, 1930
(Ballet Society, Inc.)

Tamara Toumanova in
Cotillon, 1932
(Raoul Barba/Ballet Society, Inc.)

Lincoln Kirstein in 1934
*(George Platt Lynes/Dance Collection,
New York Public Library)*

"Miss Brigitta" aged 16, 1933
(BBC Hulton Picture Library)

Balanchine with Modoc
the elephant
(United Press International)

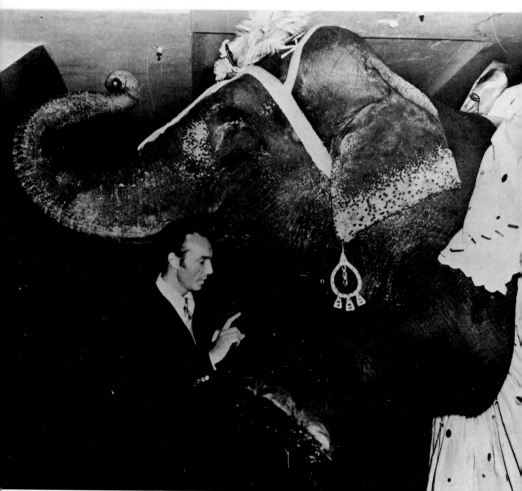

Maria Tallchief
*(Dance Collection,
New York Public Library)*

Tanaquil LeClercq in
La Valse, 1951
*(Dance Collection,
New York Public Library)*

Balanchine and Stravinsky rehearsing *Agon*, 1957 *(Martha Swope)*

Balanchine in Hamburg, 1962
(Zoë Dominic)

Suzanne Farrell and Balanchine in *Don Quixote,* 1965 *(Fred Fehl)*

Suzanne Farrell and Arthur Mitchell in *Slaughter on Tenth Avenue*
(Martha Swope)

Peter Martins as Apollo *(Martha Swope)*

Robert Irving
*(Steven Caras/New York
City Ballet)*

Jerome Robbins
(New York City Ballet)

Vienna Waltzes at the New York State Theater, 1977 *(Paul Kolnik)*

material things of life. He had made money with Cochran, and
this had continued in good measure with the Danes. He was
entering a new world and he celebrated it in dashing style.
While in Copenhagen he ordered a green Willys sports car to be
shipped from America, and it is not difficult to imagine the
pleasure it gave him, with a variety of nubile young ladies in
the passenger seat. In 1931, when he returned to London, the
car went with him to new countryside, new ladies and a new
job with Sir Oswald Stoll at the Coliseum.

Stoll was not Cochran. He presented variety shows which
featured comedians and clowns, men who played the con-
certina and dogs who performed tricks. Ninette de Valois had
danced in pantomime, Anton Dolin in the circus with sealions,
and now here was Balanchine among the trained dogs. He
collected the few dancers who were available in London and
they were billed as '16 Delightful Balanchine Girls 16'. There
was an abysmal orchestra as accompaniment, but he arranged
charming numbers and made yet more money. Now he really
did think himself London's best-dressed man, with beautiful
cravats and a bowler, the regulation Oxford 'bags', the occasional rolled umbrella and, of course, the roadster car. He even
rode in Rotten Row on Sundays – dressed, no doubt, correctly.

It was an immensely enjoyable interlude but, in 1931, only an
interlude. The Depression began to bite, and when it hit the
theatre Georges was out of work. A few weeks later, as he was
still unable to find an engagement, his resident's permit was
withdrawn. Though he longed to stay in England – he was
already devoted to London – he had no alternative but to cross
the Channel and make for Paris. For the first time in his life he
had possessions to pack and transport, and there was also the
car. He was now rather short of money, and at Calais he found
himself in an interesting situation – he could neither pay the
import duty on the car, nor the storage fees at the dock. It was
an impasse which most Britons or Americans would have
solved with a telephone call for help to the nearest friend. But
for a Georgian, and Meliton's son, there was a different solution.
He walked over to the next man standing on the quay, presented the car to him, and caught the train to Paris.

Waiting for his arrival, his somewhat neglected paramour,

Shura Danilova, was not pleased by this. She was in their Paris apartment, which Georges had not seen since the brief moment of Lifar-mania after the sanatorium. She knew about the car from letters and telephone calls and had bought some pretty green clothes to match it. The homecoming was not a success – the relationship went from bad to worse until they made a mutual decision to part. It had always been a haphazard liaison, as their careers had kept them so much apart. Both had found consoling attachments during the past year, so the decision to part was unclouded by emotional involvement. It was the most positive action they could have taken, for it enabled their long friendship from Imperial schooldays to grow closer and stronger with the years, and to the end of Balanchine's life Shura was always near him and often working with him. It became his most lasting relationship.

11

Failure

In the autumn of 1931 Balanchine received an intriguing offer;
it came from René Blum, brother of Léon Blum, the leader of the
French Socialist Party. René Blum was the new Director of the
Monte Carlo Theatre, and he was inviting Georges to be the
maître de ballet of an embryo 'Ballets Russes' which he
planned to create. It was an attractive idea, though Blum wasn't
the first to think of it: ever since Diaghilev's death rumours of a
successor company had flown between Paris and London, but
now for the first time definite plans were being made and
contracts drawn up for signature.

Balanchine jumped at the opportunity. Not only would it
take him back to Monte Carlo, but he would be working with a
full-scale company again – and from its inception, which would
give him power in the choice of dancers and repertoire. He
travelled south to meet Blum, whom he immediately liked, and
to find the designers Derain and Bérard, Boris Kochno and the
régisseur Serge Grigoriev already installed. There was another
figure on the sidelines, the villain of the piece, a former military
police and Cossack captain called Wassily Grigorievich Voskresensky, but Balanchine barely met him. At this time poor
René Blum, who was responsible for his presence, was quite
unaware of this gentleman's true nature. Revelation would
come in due course.

The first task was the recruiting of dancers for the company.
The general wish was for as many old hands from Diaghilev

days as possible, but Georges was completely against this. The last thing he wanted was a lesser replica of the original, and he stuck resolutely to his idea of combining new dancers of extreme youth in a new, exciting repertoire – exactly the view that Diaghilev would have held. In deference to the authority of Balanchine's position as ballet master, the others gave way, and he was soon on the train back to Paris to begin his search for fledgeling ballerinas. He was to be phenomenally lucky.

In the best tradition of farce, whom should he meet first – in the street – but the ancient, twenty-seven-year-old Shura Danilova. Theatrical grapevines have never been sluggish, and she knew all about the new company in Monte Carlo – except the salient point of extreme youth. She had assumed that Georges would want her services, but now found herself standing on the pavement, listening to her ex-lover telling her that she was not only 'too old' but '*much* too old'. Since even a heavyweight boxer can be fighting fit in his early thirties, this came as a shock and she was furious.

Balanchine went straight from this encounter to the studios of the two famous Maryinsky ballerinas, Olga Preobrajenska and Mathilde Kschessinska, and among the pupils he found the youth he wanted. Perhaps even he was surprised – Tatiana Riabouchinska was fourteen, Tamara Toumanova was thirteen and Irina Baronova was fully twelve years old. They were astonishing children, brought as babies from Russia when their parents escaped in the post-Revolution years. Riabouchinska possessed an unusual, ethereal quality, and Toumanova and Baronova demonstrated unnerving technical virtuosity. He snapped them up in an instant with the consent of mothers and teachers: they were to prove the greatest draw in the fortunes of the new company, and would provide him with marvellous material for his next productions.

Toumanova, beautiful and dark, and Riabouchinska, beautiful and fair, were transported to Monte Carlo, while tiny Baronova stayed in Paris to appear, with tremendous success, in a production of Offenbach's operetta *Orpheus in the Underworld*, presented at the Théâtre Mogador in December. The programme stated, 'Les Ballets Russes de Georges Balanchine', and his hastily collected dancers included Felia Doubrovska (his Diaghilev Siren) and a great *danseur noble*, Anatole Vilzak. But the twelve-year-old stole the show – 'the sensation of the evening' wrote André Levinson – and the future ballerina's career was safely launched.

Meanwhile in Monte Carlo, as 1931 ended, René Blum's company was complete and Balanchine's first production for it was something of a family affair. With G. Delaquys, Blum had written a play with music called *Les Amours du Poète* – the poet being Heinrich Heine. In Act III, to a movement of Schumann's *Carnaval*, Georges composed a dance for six admirers of the poet; its first performance was given on 5 January 1932. On 6 January he embarked on a series of opera ballets, the old Diaghilev formula for solvency, and – starting with Wagner's *Tannhäuser* and finishing with Offenbach's *La Périchole* – he completed eighteen by 31 March. Some operas he had worked on before, while others were new to him; it was an excellent way of breaking in the company, and it must have given him the opportunity to assess the talents of each individual dancer.

On 12 April the curtain rose on a ballet which, for many people, is his masterpiece: *Cotillon*. When his many detractors today dismiss Balanchine as a cold, arid technician, they surely cannot have seen this work. The music was by Emmanuel Chabrier, the slight libretto by Kochno – simply a ballroom; a young girl who tells fortunes; Fate and a Hand Gloved in Black; a Bat and a Cup of Champagne; and glorious dances for guests who include Harlequins, Jockeys and Spaniards. To my eternal regret I never saw this ballet in the theatre, but I have seen it on film – old, grainy, two-dimensional film – and it is magical. It is, however, difficult to describe as the uniqueness lies in its atmosphere, a blend of joyous youth with a strange, menacing quality, almost of tragedy. Even at the time critics spoke of it as 'haunting' and 'heart-breaking'. The setting and costumes were by Christian Bérard at his best, and Tamara Toumanova, as the Young Girl around whom the action flows, was dazzling. It is tragic that the ballet has disappeared – the last performances were given in America in 1943 – and Balanchine never again wrote anything quite like it.

On the same programme that evening was another new work

by the prolific choreographer, *La Concurrence*, followed in early May by *Le Bourgeois Gentilhomme* and *Suites de Danses*. All three had charm and style and were successful with the public. But already the dread Captain Voskresensky had made his presence felt and the atmosphere had darkened. René Blum, quiet, dignified and artistic, now realized his folly in allowing this man into the circle of management, but it was too late.

The tall, black-haired, bespectacled Captain was a shrewd manipulator of almost everything he touched and, though inartistic, he was fascinated by the theatre. He had decided that his name was altogether too cumbersome for the position, and eventual fame, that he hoped to achieve, so he assumed another – and his choice showed clearly the type of man he was. Captain became Colonel, Wassily became W, followed by the insertion of 'de' (always a bad sign), followed in turn by a short, easily remembered surname, Basil, which is the anglicized form of Wassily. As Colonel de Basil he did achieve the theatrical power he sought, and altered a number of careers in the process.

His greatest talent was for making trouble, and he fermented intrigue on a scale unknown in the ballet world of 1932. He went to work at once on poor, unsuspecting René Blum, who within a few weeks discovered that he had become a co-director with Basil and then, a month later, that he had been virtually deposed. Blum's quiet good nature and manners were no match for Basil's subtle machinations; there was even a moment of high comedy when he realized that his much-prized Rolls Royce had been bought from him by Basil with his (Blum's) own money!

Basil then turned his attention to the company, creating various factions and setting them against each other. This gave him more power over the dancers and their fortunes; it was a deeply unhappy time for many people, who had to work in a wretched atmosphere. Remembering it years later, Balanchine said, 'Basil was an octopus – a crooked octopus, and with bad taste.' He had his own problems with this man, whose tentacles were everywhere; the difficulties concerned company policy, which Basil wanted to be a mawkish mixture of sophisticated Diaghilev glamour and peasant love of Mother Russia. Shady

financial transactions were continually in the air, and to gain
his objective Basil would use any name – Balanchine's among
them – in the most cavalier fashion. Georges finally lost his
temper when he discovered that Basil had prised fifty thousand
francs from a rich young American dancer with the promise of
leading rôles in new Balanchine ballets. Implicit in this bribery
had been the suggestion that a proportion of the money would
be direct payment to the choreographer. There was quite a
scene – Georges refused to cooperate, while Basil tried to make
him see 'business sense'. The two men were now at loggerheads
over everything, and Basil, unfortunately, was in the more
powerful position.

Perhaps Balanchine should have resigned at this point; he
certainly considered doing so, but he was uncertain of the
future and delayed a decision. Basil took advantage of the lull
and made a few telephone calls. A week or two later Balanchine's own telephone rang – it was Danilova from Paris, and
she was puzzled. Why had Georges not told her he had left the
Monte Carlo company? Basil had been on the line, inviting her
to join the Ballets Russes under his new *maître de ballet*,
Léonide Massine. In this manner Balanchine discovered that he
had been sacked.

There was little to be done except pack up and leave. Derain,
Kochno and three dancers – Toumanova, Lubov Rostova and
Roman Jasinsky – left the company with him. Massine and
Danilova duly arrived and the seasons of ballet continued,
while Basil pursued his many devious paths with renewed zest.
The way in which Balanchine's removal had been engineered
was deplorable, but in the end his departure was inevitable and
right. He couldn't have continued to work with such a man, and
after the initial anger and depression he felt only relief.

He was now twenty-nine and out of work again. The prospect
was bleak and he felt responsible for the careers of the five loyal
friends who had followed him. They naturally wanted to start a
small company of their own but, with all the spirit in the world,
they realized the poverty of their situation. Nevertheless, they
started work on new ballets in Paris, where several more
dancers from Monte Carlo joined them; Balanchine,

meanwhile, kept a sharp eye open for fresh recruits from France and England. He could only pay them the barest minimum, but no one seemed to mind because of the pleasure and excitement of working with him – something I remember from Covent Garden in 1950.

By February and March of 1933 he had assembled a small repertoire though he had no idea how this would ever reach the public. Georges was his usual, fatalistic self – unspoken optimism was quite apparent in his manner – and he was rewarded by an extraordinarily quirky piece of good fortune. A rich, well-connected Englishman called Edward James came to see him. James was married to the Viennese dancer, Tilly Losch, who had appeared in the Cochran 1929 Revue: their marriage, never stable, was on the rocks again and the desperate husband was ready for desperate measures. He planned to give his wife a reconciliation present of a ballet company! Balanchine was amused, amazed and delighted – in that order. It seemed to be the salvation that he and his dancers had dreamt of through all the weeks of rehearsal.

Now there was money and the certainty of performance, and Les Ballets 1933 became a reality. André Derain was joined by Bérard, Tchelitchev and Caspar Neher; the composers Henri Sauguet, Darius Milhaud and Kurt Weill arrived with music for new productions; and Georges, his head teeming with avant-garde ideas and at his most inventive, worked his dancers until they dropped. Whether he knew it or not, word was travelling around the salons of the *haut monde* of Paris and, on the opening night of 7 June at the Théâtre des Champs Elysées, Janet Flanner of the *New Yorker* was able to write:

The French are still fond of dancing. As proof, the opening of the newly organised Les Ballets 1933 at the Champs Elysées was the most brilliant first night of tout Paris since the *ouverture* of Comte Etienne de Beaumont's 'Soirées de Paris' in '24, which was probably the most brilliant première since Diaghilev's *Sacre du Printemps* in the spring of '13. Which was probably the most brilliant début since Fanny Elssler's at the Opéra in 1834, which was probably the most brilliant first night since the court ladies of Louis XIV applauded themselves as ballet girls in Lulli's

'Triumph of Love', by special request. For four hundred years
Parisians have been regally addicted to ballet, and if the 1933
group lacked Bourbon appreciation, it enjoyed Ritz royalty,
much more tastily dressed.

That is one side of the story; here is the other, from the review of
the first night by André Levinson, the foremost French ballet
critic. Of Balanchine he wrote:

> By a phenomenon as regrettable as it is curious, this artist,
> having proved himself last year by guiding his world in the
> direction of a choreographic classicism rejuvenated by fortunate
> audacities, abdicates his role of leader and resigns himself to the
> auxiliary role of a kind of illustrator who comments, by vague
> dance steps, on the musical concepts of composers or the
> pictorial concepts of designers . . . totally disorientated, riddled
> and shaken up by contradictory esthetics . . . It is for us to hope
> that this almost total eclipse of a choreographer in whom we had
> founded the most justified hopes is only temporary; moreover it
> is necessary that he is taken in hand again by a patron capable of
> orientating his vacillating will.

As so often, these excerpts reveal more about the writer than
about the work he or she is assessing. Levinson obviously
adored the classic ballet and had found *Apollo* – and *Cotillon*,
in its different way – exactly to his taste, even in their
twentieth-century guise. He saw Balanchine as the new young
upholder of tradition, and was unwilling to recognize his
development through experiment and innovation; his view is
reminiscent of the critical reaction to the Young Ballet in Russia
years earlier. Levinson was even unable to see the classicism
underlying all those 'vague dance steps'. He was not alone in
his opinions: the chic audience of 7 June was notably luke-
warm, finding that they too were being asked to jettison their
preconceived ideas. Ironically, if Balanchine had presented the
identical ballets under the banner of Diaghilev's Ballets Russes,
the public would not only have accepted them – they would
have raved about them. And possibly Levinson would have
raved too.

The programme which caused such disappointment

consisted of three ballets: *Mozartiana*, to the Suite No. 4 by Tchaikovsky, with setting and costumes by Bérard and a front curtain showing Mozart as a child at the harpsichord; *Les Songes*, with music by Milhaud and décor and costumes by Derain, who also provided the theme, that of a fêted ballerina falling asleep in her bedroom, being assailed by nightmare and waking to her flowers, reality and relief; and lastly *The Seven Deadly Sins* by Kurt Weill and Bertolt Brecht, with Caspar Neher as designer. This was certainly an interesting programme, with Toumanova and Jasinsky in the first ballets, and the singer Lotte Lenya and the dancer-mime Tilly Losch as the two 'Annas' in the Weill–Brecht.

There were three more ballets in the repertoire, enough for a second complete programme. *Fastes* with a score by Sauguet and book, setting and costumes by Derain (the book consisted of various jolly happenings at an Etruscan feast), *L'Errante*, to Schubert's marvellous 'Wanderer' Fantasy, with book, set, costumes and spectacular lighting by Pavel Tchelitchev; the central character was played by Tilly Losch and the programme states 'Miss Losch's dress by the House of Molyneux' – perhaps yet another conciliatory present from poor husband James? Last *Les Valses de Beethoven* – which included one of his Scottish songs – orchestrated by Nicholas Nabokov, who became a great friend of Balanchine, and with designs by Emilio Terry. The theme was the Greek myth of Apollo and Daphne (Jasinsky and Tilly Losch) and, as two of the Elements, Balanchine chose two English girls – Diana Gould as Earth and Prudence Hyman as Air. Fire was danced by Tamara Sidorenko and, as Water, T. Ouchkova – pronounce it how you like, surely an unhappy name for a dancer!

The Paris season was off to a bad start, and after Levinson's review the theatre was never more than half full for any performance. Worse, the rival Monte Carlo company arrived for a season at the Théâtre Châtelet, where Diaghilev had given his first Ballets Russes season with Astruc in 1909. Basil proceeded to have a tremendous success with his dancers, and much was written about the great improvement in the company since their last Paris appearance – when Balanchine had been ballet master. He must have felt sick at heart as one blow followed another, but, as every performer knows, when the public is apathetic there is nothing to be done except soldier on in hope. And, luckily, Balanchine seems to have had little capacity for bitterness in his nature.

On 28 June Les Ballets 1933 opened their second and final short season, at the Savoy Theatre in London. The repertoire contained one addition, a ballet by Lifar in which he danced with Alice Nikitina. Public reaction was similar to that of Paris and, when Basil's company opened to public acclaim at the Alhambra on 4 July, the Savoy was almost empty. In a matter of days it was clear that it was all over: the season closed, the company disbanded and Edward James was the poorer by over a million francs. He was soon to lose Tilly Losch in a noisy and scandalous divorce suit – poor man, it had certainly *not* been his year.

From all the contemporary reviews it would seem that this company had been an artistic as well as a financial failure. But a number of expert people are still alive in London and New York who saw the 1933 performance and who still think them among the most original and fascinating in the ballet theatre. Agnes de Mille, then a student with Marie Rambert at the tiny Mercury Theatre, was deeply impressed by the ideas and choreographic invention. And both Ninette de Valois and Frederick Ashton are unstinting in their admiration and praise for Balanchine's achievement with this small group. Neither are notably uncritical of Balanchine, either professionally or personally, but when speaking of his 1933 productions they wax almost lyrical. They were both in London that summer at the Sadler's Wells Theatre where de Valois had launched her English school and company. Each speaks of attending the Savoy night after night, so they must have seen the same ballets many times. Neither thinks that the repertoire of Basil's company could compare with the miniature gems on view at the Savoy – to rows of empty seats. Fred Ashton particularly admired *L'Errante* and *The Seven Deadly Sins*, though for him no Balanchine ballet ever quite touched the magic of *Cotillon*.

Another occasional member of Balanchine's sparse audience was Nijinsky's Hungarian wife, Romola. She was a determined, predatory little woman whom I saw frequently in the later

thirties when she brought Vaslav's daughter, Kyra, to classes at
Nicholas Legat's studio. Kyra was in my class, though a few
years older. She was startlingly like her father at that time but,
sadly, without her father's genius for the dance. Even at ten
years old I felt embarrassed and upset by her mother's efforts to
force her into the ballet. Now, in 1933, Nijinsky was lan-
guishing in a Swiss sanatorium and Romola had written a book
about her life with him. She had been assisted in her task by a
rich young American called Lincoln Kirstein, whose love for
the art of ballet had become a passion. Together they attended
one of the last Savoy performances when Georges danced in
L'Errante in place of the injured Roman Jasinsky. At the fall of
the final curtain Romola took the thirty-year-old, six-foot-three-
inch American to the stage door and to meet Balanchine in his
dressing room. They found him, miserably depressed and
exhausted, sitting at his dressing table, staring into space.

Part 3

12
Lincoln Kirstein

It was a cold January morning in 1985. For the third time I was in New York for research, questioning and listening to Balanchine's friends and colleagues and I set out from the Algonquin Hotel for my last interview. It would be different from all my previous encounters, as I wanted to talk to Lincoln Kirstein about his own life. He was the man who had brought Balanchine to America in 1933; he had written, often and at length, about his balletmaster, but he himself had remained a shadowy figure. On the way to Lincoln Center I tried to clear my mind of all that I had heard about this rich American, but it was difficult: 'You never know where you are with him'; 'One minute he's warm and full of charm, the next cold and withdrawn'; 'A bit mad, you know'; 'Ripe for the funny farm'. I couldn't remember if we had ever met. I had a hazy memory of shaking hands with a tall, distinctive-looking man at a reception in 1949, when the Sadler's Wells company gave their first American season at the old Metropolitan Opera House, but nothing more.

At the School of American Ballet I found myself in lifts and corridors with young ballet students in varying stages of après-class disarray. I felt out of place – the situation seemed so remote, so forgotten, that I might have been a visiting scientist or professor of history. Lincoln Kirstein was waiting for me at the door of his office – smiling, diffident and alarming all at once. Now nearing eighty, he had not allowed age to shrink his stature. He reminded me of a great, stooped bird, a secretary

bird, angular and predatory. As we went into his comfortable
office I was given an example of perfect good manners, the
particular brand that you find in a cultivated East Coaster,
when natural authority is combined with courteous behaviour
in a relaxed, amused way. Manners are indefinable. Sadly
unfashionable today, they never played any part in the English
ballet world that I remember, which could be ill-mannered to
the point of crudeness. Perhaps I lay too much stress on them –
one notices them instinctively or one doesn't – but I remember
how Balanchine's innate good manners affected me from the
moment of our meeting, and now, with Lincoln Kirstein, it was
the same.

However, this was not a time for relaxation, as I realized at
once. Leaning forward with a grim expression, my subject said,
'How can you write? What do you know? You don't know the
repertory.' This last statement was revealing, and throughout
the next hour he made it clear that he thought of Balanchine,
and any book about him, solely in terms of ballets, choreography and his teaching. As I murmured that I was principally
interested in attempting a portrait of a man, a sarcastic gleam
appeared, 'Oh, I see, one of those gossipy books – well, they
don't interest me.' There were several things I would like to
have said in reply, but I rejected them all. He was right about
the repertoire – how could I know it with the close daily
involvment he considered necessary? But perhaps he was
ignoring the fact that a dancer can see and understand a choreographer's development in a way that a non-dancer never
can? This wasn't the moment for argument so instead I decided
to make him laugh and, with luck, lighten and prolong an
interview which showed every sign of disintegration. Success
was immediate. In next to no time this forbidding man was
chortling like a schoolboy. Indiscretions tumbled from him
about anyone and anything. His capacity for gossip was both
feminine and feline; while enjoying it greatly, I reflected on his
earlier remark and, indeed, on the disgracefully libellous copy
he was giving me.

He had said, when we first met, that on no account would he
talk about himself; but now I asked him to tell me about his
early life – which he did, though hesitantly, leaving me to fill in

the gaps. His start in life was exceptional. He was born in Rochester, New York, into a rich Jewish family who moved to Boston when he was five years old. His varied artistic talents were given help and encouragement: he played the piano well, painted well, was rich enough to buy his first picture at the age of ten and saw Pavlova dance when he was twelve. At fourteen he had written and published a play; at fifteen he spent the summer in London, meeting the famous Bloomsbury set and no doubt falling under the spell of the effervescent Lydia Lopokova Keynes. And at seventeen he saw Diaghilev's Ballets Russes for the first time and felt he had found the right direction for his life.

From 1924 to 1929 he was in Europe each summer, becoming obsessed with the ballet and also, I think, with Diaghilev. While at Harvard he emulated the great impresario's early life by publishing articles on painting and photography; by co-founding the Harvard Society for Contemporary Arts, and by editing an excellent literary quarterly, *Hound and Horn*. He was in Venice during the stifling August of 1929, looking at pictures and enjoying being young, rich and independent. One morning, in San Giorgio dei Greci, he found himself unwittingly caught up in the funeral service for someone of obvious importance. Later, in London, he read a description of that service for Sergey Diaghilev – and he was both troubled and thrilled that fate should have led him to it.

He said little about relations within his family, but it became obvious that he was not on the happiest of terms with his father. He gave momentary hints about his behaviour and mode of life at this time, not calculated to endear him to any family, and I formed an impression of a wilful, spoiled boy and a father deeply out of sympathy with the habits and predilections of the ballet world. I asked him directly, 'As your father was so antagonistic to everything you were enjoying, why did he give you your full inheritance as you were leaving Harvard?'

He answered immediately, 'Because of what I said I'd do if he didn't.' Then, as if in explanation, he leaned forward with a most curious expression on his face – a mixture of malevolence and amusement – and, in his delightful East Coast drawl, said, 'I was not a very nice little boy.'

I liked him so much at that moment. That was endearing – so honest, so direct. I could see the beautiful house in Boston, the Jewish family of immense stability and convention, and this one 'peculiarly' artistic son who might well bring shame upon them. He was not a nice little boy, but he grew up to become a man of fascinating character, with charm and a refreshingly honest self-perception.

When we talked about the ballet, I was struck by the curiously divisive attitude that one sometimes finds in the very rich. He spoke continually of 'rich kids' and 'poor kids', believing that all talent lies in what he termed 'the working class'. He is proud of the fact that the New York City Ballet employs so many from this background, pointing his finger firmly at the Royal Ballet in London, and at Ninette de Valois in particular. He is convinced that she always refused to have that 'class' in her company; no matter that I told him this was nonsense, he simply wasn't listening! As to 'rich kids' – it was amusing to hear him speak of his friend Edward Warburg, of the banking family, a Harvard boy who had helped to found the Contemporary Arts Society. In Lincoln's words, 'Oh, he was a rich kid, the youngest of seven and with nothing to do. He had some interest in painting but none for the ballet – I just took his money and so did George.' Warburg's money did much to establish Balanchine in America in the thirties and early forties.

So to Georges, or George, himself. He emerged, in the words of his collaborator, as a wonderfully talented machine, without hint of flesh, bone or life blood. Kirstein made one sly personal reference to him, containing a little barb for me: 'Of course you'll want to know about his seven [sic] wives, and all those he didn't marry' – exactly the sort of gossipy remark he had earlier deplored. As I made no reply he returned to his picture of an automaton spewing out ballet steps and patterns twelve hours a day, painting a self-portrait as he did so.

His passion has always been the school, the first School of American Ballet, his baby. It is a great school, brought to its standard of perfection by Balanchine's teaching, and it produces an apparently never-ending flow of top-class ballerinas and *danseurs nobles*. But this enviable standard has caused him to under-rate European achievements. 'The Russians are standing still; the Danes are standing still' – he didn't even mention France and Italy, who have the oldest schools of all – 'and the English have no school at all.' Again I was silent, but from a mixture of embarrassment and misplaced loyalty, as I have no connection with the English school. There was some truth in his final generalization; English classical ballet is at one of its lowest ebbs, and only a radical change of style, attitude and policy can save it.

I enjoyed my meeting with Lincoln Kirstein. He is stimulating, amusing, cultivated and rather unbalanced – an unusual American dilettante. His relationship with Balanchine over fifty years must have been a strange one, an odd couple indeed. In spite of his occasionally intimidating exterior – beetle brows lowering over piercing hawk eyes – I tend to believe a phrase that I have heard from many people, 'Balanchine always got everything he wanted from Lincoln.' As I was leaving he swooped into his outer office for a copy of his book, *Portrait of Mr B.*, which he presented charmingly. I already had a copy but received it, I hope, gracefully. Alas, his writing is not for me: we are in Edwin Denby-land again, only more so, for Kirstein's considerable erudition is given an airing in almost every sentence. I cannot imagine an ordinary member of the public staggering through to the end of his long essay which is a pity as he has much to say which is illuminating.

There was a morale-boosting, happy final moment as he said, 'George mentioned you often – oh yes, he talked about you a lot', and from his expression I felt it could not have been all bad.

When Lincoln Kirstein entered Balanchine's dressing room at the Savoy Theatre in 1933, little was said – the choreographer was in no shape to hold more than the simplest conversation. But when they met again a few days later in a London hotel, the young American poured out his vision of a great ballet company in the New World. It fell on receptive ears: Balanchine's disillusionment with Europe was complete and his own thoughts were straying across the Atlantic, not discouraged by the attractions of Miss Ginger Rogers on the silver screen. Could all American girls look so terrific?! In spite of the difference in temperament between these two men they liked each other, and

a common goal cemented their friendship. Balanchine had no
ties in Europe and he made a willing and immediate decision,
with only one condition – that Vladimir Dimitriev, his original
Russian benefactor, should accompany him and become
administrator of the new School of American Ballet. His loyalty
to his friend was absolute.

They sailed on the old liner *Olympic*, arriving in New York
on 18 October. In a ferment of artistic enthusiasm Lincoln
Kirstein had already secured the time and money of Edward
Warburg, and together they had planned and effected a setting
and facilities for the school which to them seemed ideal. It was
situated in Hartford, Connecticut, in the environs of the Morgan
Memorial Museum which had an excellent auditorium and
classrooms, and everything was ready for the arrival of the
Russians from England. Both Americans were certain that
Balanchine would be overjoyed to be working in such tranquil,
spacious conditions; but the amateur can never know exactly
what the professional needs.

George's reaction was inevitable – he was angered and
confused. Where was New York, the big city, the centre? From
St Petersburg, through western Europe to London, he had
always worked in big cities, usually capital cities and, more
often than not, in opera houses. What was this small provincial
town, this apparent backwater? Was this the best the great
American continent could do? He felt so lost, so let down, that
he would have returned to Europe but for the odd trick that fate
frequently plays.

Tuberculosis struck again, seriously, and George lay wretch-
edly ill for many weeks. A Russian doctor had been found who
prescribed a mysterious treatment – the consumption of as
much food as a human being can take. Pints of cream, pounds of
butter, rounds of cheese coursed down his gullet, and he gained
thirty pounds in as many days. It sounds extraordinary but it
worked; he recovered to find Hartford a thing of the past, and in
its place a dismal classroom – once used by Isadora Duncan –
on Madison Avenue and 59th Street in the centre of New York.
It was not the largesse he had expected from the New World,
but the studio had the right smell, the right feel, and it was *his*.
He knew he could work from such a beginning.

So it began, on 1 January 1934, with twenty-five pupils.

Dimitriev was the director, Balanchine the chairman, with a board consisting of two teachers, Dorothie Littlefield for the juniors and a former *danseur noble*, Pierre Vladimirov. Vladimirov had succeeded Nijinsky at the Maryinsky, had partnered Pavlova with the greatest distinction, and was the husband of Balanchine's tall 'Siren', Felia Doubrovska. The twenty-five young pupils did not know how lucky they were to receive training from two such teachers as Vladimirov and Balanchine. One of them, the sixteen-year-old Ruthanna Boris, gave a charming quote to Bernard Taper many years later:

> We were all shy with Balanchine. He was a great figure to us, and handsome. He had beautiful sideburns. Most of us instantly decided we were in love with him. He asked me to do a double turn. I said I couldn't. 'Certainly you can,' he said. I got halfway around when suddenly I felt a whack on my behind, and I spun all the way around before I fell down in surprise. It was the first time in my dance training that anyone had laid a hand on me. Our training hitherto had been aloof, impersonal, very proper. That wasn't the Russian way which involved whacking, pushing, tugging, touching, poking, lots of physical contact. It was a whole different way of communicating, and very electrifying. Suddenly I found myself doing things I had never thought possible.

That passage takes me back vividly to my own training with Nicholas Legat, and subsequently with his widow, Nadine Nicolaeva. And the earthy manhandling extended to speech as well. 'Squeeze your lemons!' she would shout when buttocks were not drawn tightly together and, to one dancer whose head was not dipped as it should be, 'More – *more – smell your armpeet*'!

It has been said and written many times that Balanchine was the one and only choice for Lincoln Kirstein as he dreamed of a great American school and ballet company. Vera Zorina, the second Mrs Balanchine and a protégée of Léonide Massine, disagrees and says, 'Lincoln would have taken *any* choreographer.' Whatever the truth, George was the available one – disillusioned, down and out, and ready for change – and through Lincoln Kirstein's urgency and obsessive vision the arts in America have been marvellously enriched.

13
Metropolitan Opera

Balanchine liked America. He felt relaxed in the free and easy, open atmosphere, something he had never found in Russia and western Europe, and in spite of the small, rather dreary surroundings of his school he worked tirelessly, knowing that he was creating a unique institution. He possessed an essential quality in an outstanding teacher, the ability to use even the most unlikely human material in a constructive way.

There can be no better example of this than the occasion when, after six months, he decided to whip his students into shape for a performance of a new ballet he would write specially for them. It was a private 'by invitation' performance and it took place at Woodlands, the estate of Felix Warburg, father of Edward, near White Plains in New York State. A photograph of a rehearsal survives which demonstrates perfectly this quality in Balanchine. The young women pictured are Amazons. They remind one irresistibly of John Betjeman's '. . . Pam, you great big mountainous sports girl whizzing them over the net, full of the strength of five'! In addition to this Junoesquery he had another problem. Sometimes seventeen girls would appear for a rehearsal, sometimes nine, then six, then a few unexpected stray boys, and so on. One girl flew in terribly late one evening, while another suddenly fell on her knees and burst into tears. Balanchine made use of every episode and situation, choreographing them into the finished ballet.

Surprisingly, this ballet – *Serenade*, to the first three movements of Tchaikovsky's String Serenade in C – became almost a signature tune for Balanchine. He adapted and changed it many times in later years, when he had achieved his goal of a sophisticated, beautifully shaped and technically expert company. But the original foundations were always there, stemming from that funny, motley group in the White Plains photograph. What he had tried to do, he said later, was to give these raw young students an idea of how dull, difficult classroom exercises could be transmuted into a performance of grace and beauty. The number of dancers on stage at any given time didn't matter: the choreography was a pattern of pure dancing with many arrivals and departures, so that the late girl and the weeping girl were quite acceptable. In addition he had arranged combinations of steps which would disguise inadequacies and inexpert technique, giving each dancer the chance to appear elegant and physically controlled. No doubt this seems sensible enough, but it is rare. If one wanted a single example of Balanchine's pre-eminence over all other choreographers, it is in the making of *Serenade*.

During the remaining months of 1934 two notable Americans became interested in George's work. Nelson Rockefeller gave financial assistance to the school and, with the prospect of a first small company, Mrs W. K. Vanderbilt and some of her friends did the same. Behind the scenes hovered the quiet, rather gloomy presence of Dimitriev: a shadowy figure in the memories of those who knew him, managing the school and arrangements for the new company well enough, keeping a paternal eye on George's interests, but never happy with Kirstein and Warburg, whom he considered dilettante and amateur. He soldiered on until 1940 when, financial disagreements becoming acute, he was bought out by Lincoln Kirstein and his association with the ballet ended.

Balanchine's first attempt with a small professional company – the American Ballet – took place in New York at the Adelphi Theater in March 1935. Twenty-six advanced students from the school were his entire complement, and he brought in two more experienced guest dancers, Tamara Geva and Paul Haakon. The fact that Tamara was his ex-wife was neither here nor there: George seemed able to work amicably with all his dancers, no matter what the past relationship, and he always inspired complete loyalty. In view of his fairly extensive marital, and extra-marital, activities, this was quite an achievement.

He presented six ballets – *Serenade*, together with three other new works, and two from the repertoire of Les Ballets 1933. The public were apathetic, and so were the critics. Indeed the leading American dance critic, John Martin of *The New York Times*, was strongly antagonistic, attacking Balanchine's choreography as 'precious' and 'decadent', calling it 'Riviera aesthetics' and suggesting that the American Ballet would have a better future if Balanchine returned to Europe and stayed there (an amusing suggestion, as the company owed its very existence to Balanchine). Martin would continue in this vein for many years, finding little or nothing to praise even when the public was showing enthusiasm. The *volte-face* that he later had to perform, when the choreographer had become an acknowledged master, must have caused him pain.

The two-week engagement at the Adelphi came to an end with the minimum of public interest. While the school continued to establish itself, and several students began to acquire the style and technical virtuosity that their teachers demanded, Balanchine, Kirstein and Warburg made an ill-considered decision – to take this inexperienced troupe on a fourteen-week tour of the North American continent. That Kirstein and Warburg wanted to do this does not surprise me, but Balanchine's agreement does: it suggests a lapse of judgement comparable to his performance of Nijinsky's *Spectre de la Rose* in Copenhagen in 1930. In the event, the tour was a complete disaster – the theatre manager suffered a nervous breakdown and there wasn't enough money to cover expenses. They had only reached Scranton, Pennsylvania, when the chastened little group was forced to limp back to New York. This failure added fuel to the jaundiced view already held by John Martin and by a section of the public.

Balanchine's optimistic outlook might have taken a deserved knock at this point but luck, or what appeared to be luck, was at hand. Edward Johnson, the former singer and new director of

the Metropolitan Opera House, invited the American Ballet and
its balletmaster to become resident with the opera company in
the old house. For George, this was the realization of his dream;
he would be in a Maryinsky environment again and with the
opportunity of staging productions of style and scale. He didn't
hesitate. He knew nothing of the morgue-like atmosphere of the
Met; of the long and gloomy dictatorship of Giulio Gatti-
Casazza, or of the calibre of his successor. All he could hear
were Johnson's honeyed words of bringing 'freshness, youth
and novelty to the Metropolitan', and he could see his (now
slimmer) long-legged American students doing just that.

He knew he would be expected to churn out one opera ballet
after another, and this is exactly what happened. Between 16
and 27 December his dances were performed in *La Traviata,
Faust, Aïda, Lakmé, Tannhäuser, Carmen* and *Rigoletto,*
followed in early January by *Mignon, Manon, La Juive* and *La
Rondine.* He felt these were small tasks in return for evenings of
his own ballets. Not for an instant did he realize that there
could be two entirely different interpretations of the agreement.

Disillusionment came gradually. The cramped dressing
rooms given to the dancers were in the Met basement, and soon
the management started to complain about everything: they
wore out too many pairs of shoes, and their costumes had to be
cleaned too often; their style was wrong, much too showy for
the opera and as for expecting to rehearse on the stage – and
with orchestra – no, no, a piano in a hall somewhere was quite
sufficient. All the work George poured into the opera ballets
met with nothing but dissension from the management and
failure with the public. Perhaps this failure was partly his own
fault. He was unable to tailor his vigorous, inventive style to the
slow, dreary, old-fashioned style of the opera productions, and
the clash between the two was obvious to everyone.

The greatest blow was the discovery that Edward Johnson
had no intention of allowing full evenings of ballet. The reason
given was always the same – no money available for the extra
orchestra rehearsals which would be required. But George was
nothing if not ingenious: he learned of the non-operatic music
in the orchestra's repertoire and set to work to create ballets
which would need the minimum of the orchestra's time. These

he was allowed to present – doing so to increasing public interest and acclaim. He gave one of his leading dancers, William Dollar, the chance to choreograph his first ballet – *Concerto*, to Chopin's Piano Concerto in F Minor. John Martin was invited to attend a final piano rehearsal, but such was the opinion of dance and dancers in the old Metropolitan that he was turned away at the door – even the doorman thought that critics only came to the opera. Martin's temper at that moment was not recorded.

Balanchine's own temper was being severely tested during these weeks and months. He was happy to be in America, he liked Americans and he loved New York. But he was restless. He continually moved from apartment to apartment on the East Side of the city – furnishing each one and making it comfortable, then leaving and starting the whole process again somewhere else. He made many friends; they found him quite without the nostalgia for Russia and Europe that plagued their relationships with other Europeans, but beneath his charm and humour they detected detachment and loneliness. I find it revealing that all his close friends were Russians – Pavel Tchelitchev, Vladimir Dukelsky and Nicolas Nabokov from Diaghilev days; his rehearsal pianist, Nicholas Kopeikine, and a dancer, George Volodine. They spoke in their own language. When Balanchine bought a small car they often drove out to Long Island and Connecticut at weekends – in search of what? Restaurants where they could drink glasses of Russian tea. In spite of all his protestations of being 'at home' in America, I am sure that nostalgia – even homesickness – for his own country, people and customs played a far greater part in Balanchine's life than he cared to show to the world.

One aspect of himself which he did show during the months of strain at the Met was unwise and damaging: he allowed his contempt both for the management and for some published criticism to become all too obvious. Bernard Taper quotes his reply to a complaint from Johnson that his opera ballets had no respect for tradition – 'Of course not. The tradition of the ballet at the Met is bad ballet.' He had continued by comparing their use of ballet in opera to a diner using a napkin and wiping his mouth before resuming his meal. His own aim was to create dances which would be tasty dishes in their own right.

More damaging still was his extraordinary reply to a newspaper reporter who asked him how dancers adapted to working with a full opera company. 'Generally,' he said, 'I instructed my dancers to dance all over the place. The dancers must pay no attention to the singing chorus. I advised them to kick the chorus if they got in the way.' He lashed out at music critics, declaring that they knew nothing about the ballet and precious little about music. None of this endeared him to the public or management, and certainly not to the critics. These were the first signs of intolerance in Balanchine which, sadly, became more apparent with age.

It seemed certain that the American Ballet and the Met management would part company, with mutual relief, at the close of the 1935 season. But Edward Johnson, who planned a spring season at popular prices, offered Balanchine the chance to choreograph and stage Gluck's *Orpheus and Eurydice* as a ballet, with décor and costumes by Pavel Tchelitchev. General amazement and some cynical assessment were expressed for the reasons behind such an apparently generous offer – Lincoln Kirstein was not slow to suggest that this might be the Met's malicious way of causing Balanchine to commit suicide in public. Whatever the reasons, George was excited by the project; so was the effervescent designer, and the ubiquitous Warburg promised once again to share the production costs.

Tchelitchev's avant-garde ideas were the mainspring for the production which now took shape, though, as always, the mainspring for Balanchine was the musical score – and this opera had been a favourite for many years. Kirstein, hypnotized by the strong-willed designer, wrote a programme note stressing the presentation of the Orpheus legend in modern, 1936 terms. For 'the eternal domestic tragedy of an artist and his wife ... We saw Hell as a concentration camp with flying military slave-drivers lashing forced labour; the Elysian Fields as an ether drama, a desiccated bone-dry limbo of suspended animation, and Paradise as the eternity we know from a Planetarium arrayed on the astronomical patterns of contemporary celestial science.' This is Lincoln Kirstein in super-heated vein but, concentrating solely on the facts within his text, was this the

moment in the American Ballet's association with the Met to
mount such a calculatedly outrageous production?

The première was scheduled for 19 May 1936. America's first
danseur noble, Lew Christensen, handsome and talented, was
cast as Orpheus, Daphne Vane as Eurydice, and William Dollar
as Amor. With the singers and chorus safely tucked away with
the orchestra in the pit, the curtain rose. Soon it was clear that a
major theatrical disaster was in progress. The public hated it;
the critics hated it (and were savage in their reviews); the Met
management took one look, allowed one further performance
and withdrew it from the repertoire. Although an occasional
faint word of praise for both the ballet and the principals could
be heard, this was drowned in the general condemnation –
Balanchine and the American Ballet were a failure. But it was
failure on the grand scale – which is, after all, the next best
thing to success on the grand scale. Nothing in the theatre is
worse than timid failure.

Surprisingly, the Met association continued. Morale among
the dancers sank lower and lower but Balanchine, with Warburg's money alone, staged one final fling in the old opera
house – an all-Stravinsky gala evening. It was held on 27 April
1937: the ballets presented were *Apollo*, the new *Baiser de la
Fée*, and the new *Card Game – a Ballet in Three Deals*, to a
score commissioned by Kirstein and Warburg. Stravinsky came
to conduct seventy players from the New York Philharmonic,
replacing the Met orchestra to avoid a further clash with the
management, and the public and critical success was as great as
the disaster of *Orpheus*. Critics went so far as to describe it as
the most brilliant evening of ballet ever seen in New York. It
was a triumphant moment for George and his young dancers,
but only a moment; the next day brought them back to the
dispiriting operatic grind.

Within a few weeks Edward Warburg decided that he had
had enough, which was not surprising as he had lost one
hundred thousand dollars in three years. Balanchine and his
doomed company held on until March 1938, when the Met
connection was finally severed. As he left, George gave a last
blast to the press: 'The Met is a heap of ruins, and every night
the stagehands put it together and make it look a little like
opera.'

14
Brigitta

The American Ballet was no more, but Balanchine had other strings to his bow during his association with the Metropolitan Opera. While he was devising ballets for twenty-two operas and presenting new works of his own, he had been wooed and won by the New York commercial theatre. With his startling capacity for work, he had no difficulty in dividing his energies between the Met and a series of musical comedies for various Broadway theatres. It was not always work which meant a great deal to him, but he was interested and attracted by a new form of choreography, and one which held the possible reward of immediate public success.

His first 'show' was the *Ziegfeld Follies* of 1936, with music by his friend Vladimir Dukelsky now Americanized as Vernon Duke, and lyrics by Ira Gershwin. The original funny girl, Fanny Brice, was the star – there was a young man with a comic nose called Bob Hope, and an eccentric, black star performer from France with a beautiful body, Josephine Baker. She was, of course, American, but France had made her a star. She not only possessed a natural, un-selfconscious talent and a lovely singing voice, but also the most celebrated bottom of the 1930s, and George was given the task of arranging dance numbers to enhance this. Though his efforts didn't set New York on fire, the result was pleasing enough and there was piquancy in his simultaneous assignment at the Met – dances for Wagner's *Die Meistersinger*.

The Follies led to something more important – a new show with book, music and lyrics by Richard Rodgers, Lorenz Hart and George Abbot. They were distinguished men in the musical comedy business and it is interesting to read of Richard Rodgers' feelings about his new colleague:

> I expected fiery temperament. He had bushy black hair, gleaming eyes and an acquiline profile. He was Russian, artistic, a genius. I was scared stiff of him. I asked him how he worked. Did he make the steps first and have music written to fit them, or what? He answered, in the thick Russian accent he had then, 'You write, I put on.' For me, this was marvellous. I went ahead and wrote the score, and I never had to change or cut a note of it as far as he was concerned.

Later after several shows together, Rodgers added:

> He was a pleasure to work with – untemperamental, logical, objective. In all the shows I worked on with him, I never once heard him speak above a normal conversational tone – not even when everybody else was succumbing to hysteria. With most other choreographers I've known, it was like asking them to give up some of their living flesh if they were told that, for one reason or another, one of their dance numbers wouldn't work. But Balanchine would just take it in his stride and cheerfully produce on the spot any number of perfectly brilliant ideas to take the place of what came out.

The show was *On Your Toes*, with Tamara Geva and the remarkable Ray Bolger in the leading rôles. Instantly successful, it was notable for a new integration of plot and dance – a seamless production where dances and ballets arose naturally from the story line. Perhaps because of this, Balanchine asked if his programme credit could be 'Choreography by . . .' instead of the usual 'Dances by . . .'; though hesitant, the management agreed, and this innovation was to become standard theatrical practice. Within two years Vera Zorina took over the principal rôle in the London production; by all accounts she was not as good a dancer as Tamara Geva but a much better actress, and she also made the film of the musical which was released in 1939.

Now, fifty years on, this show has been revived, first in New York and then in London. I saw the opening night at the Palace Theatre in London and was disappointed and saddened. Where was the style, the elegance and the zip we had all heard so much about? In spite of acclaim and awards, the leading performers were two-dimensional and rather vulgar and the show had dated beyond repair. For the first time I understood an often repeated maxim of Balanchine's, one that had always puzzled me – that ballets were like butterflies, not built to last, and that there should always be completely new invention with each new era. That was what was wrong with this revival, and if only Balanchine could have been there I am certain that he would have reworked the entire choreography to suit the style of the 1980s.

George had not met Vera Zorina when she first appeared in *On Your Toes*. Born Eva Brigitta Hartwig in Berlin, of Norwegian stock, she was twenty years old and very beautiful in the Nordic, Garboesque style which was so admired in the 1930s. She had been a member of the Ballets Russes de Monte Carlo, when Léonide Massine took her under his wing, and today she is amusing about the way in which she was rechristened. As Hartwig was not considered suitable she was shown a list of long Russian names, arranged alphabetically, and told to choose one. As her eyes travelled down the page she realized that she couldn't pronounce any of then, till – right at the bottom – she saw an easy one, Zorina. The Vera which subsequently preceded it was simply for programmes and the press – she has always remained Brigitta to colleagues and friends.

She was not a great dancer but she was supremely elegant, stylish, individual and of high intelligence. People were fascinated by her, and during her London success in *On Your Toes* Sam Goldwyn was not slow to sign her up for a new movie he planned to present, *The Goldwyn Follies*. He was also aware of the manner in which George Balanchine was transforming the American musical in New York – there was now another Rodgers–Hart–Balanchine success at the Shubert Theater, *Babes in Arms* – so George was also signed to choreograph ballets for the Follies movie. *Babes in Arms* was notable for another Balanchine innovation, the first 'dream' ballet in a musical show. His ideas and choreographic invention for this were so successful with the public that dream ballets in popular shows became *de rigueur* for many years.

For him, these were hectic days. The dismal operatic grind at the Met, the Stravinsky Gala to arrange and organize, the taxing work in the commercial theatre, and now Hollywood and a new medium. Balanchine was in his element, with ideas tumbling from him day and night. He was excited by the prospect of California – would Miss Ginger Rogers be waiting for him? And there was another reason for his pleasure; he was making a lot of money.

Hollywood did not disappoint him; it offered an ideal climate for his health, with sunshine, colour and scores of nubile, long-legged American girls. He met Goldwyn and suffered a little, as everyone did who tried to work with Goldwyn; he met George Gershwin, who had already written songs for the movie and who was about to start work on the ballet score. But the composer became ill, even before their second meeting, and grew weaker and more helpless as the weeks passed. The score was never written and Gershwin never returned to New York – he died from a brain tumour at the age of thirty-eight. It was a great shock to Balanchine.

When rehearsals for the film began, George worked with the twenty-five dancers of the American Ballet whom he had insisted on bringing from the East Coast; and his new leading lady joined them. She was twenty, he was thirty-three, and he fell desperately in love with her – real love, I believe, for the only time in his life, because with her he fell in love with a woman and not with her work. Brigitta was a great influence in his life for many years. I don't think it is too fanciful to suggest that their relationship was as crucial to his development as the early abandonment by his family in Russia and his loneliness and fear during the Revolution.

For the missing Gershwin ballet music in the film, George decided to use the *American in Paris* score. His head filled with cinematic ideas, he dragooned his dancers in complex choreography, and when he was finally satisfied with the result he summoned Goldwyn to the set. It was a moment of pure farce: the great theatre choreographer with every conceivable camera angle, high, low and upside down, and the great film mogul expecting comfortable, traditional ballet from a safe seat in the stalls! After old Sam had been dragged round his own studio, peering through cameras from crouching, squatting and prone positions, he made a scene. Finally he stalked out in one direction, George in the other, and there was deadlock. Eventually a conventional *Water-nymph Ballet* (shades of *Swan Lake*) was substituted, for which Balanchine had arranged suitably conventional choreography. Goldwyn promised him full cinematic rein for his ideas in a future production, but inevitably this never took place. Everything that happened during the filming of the Follies was in the true spirit of Goldwyn megalomania – infuriating at the time, but hugely enjoyable in retrospect.

Back in New York, the early months of 1938 were filled with preparations for a new Rodgers and Hart musical called *I Married an Angel*, with Brigitta as Angel. George was blissfully happy, more in love with her than ever, and with her his life changed greatly. He started to enjoy his money, spending it with ease and flair. He bought a grand apartment on Central Park South and built a house on Long Island; he owned one of the first MGs seen in New York and there were champagne parties night after night. Fewer Russians surrounded him now, and many more New Yorkers. The show opened at the Shubert Theater on 11 May and enjoyed the almost statutory success expected from this team of composer, lyricist and choreographer. It was still running the following Christmas and into 1939.

While Brigitta appeared nightly at the Shubert, Balanchine worked on two further musicals – *The Boys from Syracuse* with Rodgers and Hart and *Great Lady* with Frederick Loewe and Earle Crooker. Among his dancers in the latter's cast were two famous names, Nora Kaye and André Eglevsky. (When I was ten, Eglevsky – perhaps seventeen or eighteen then – took classes at Legat's studio. One day he picked me up and threw me high in the air in a mock pas de deux. I nearly died with excitement and loved him dearly ever after – it's a strangely vivid memory.)

These two shows opened in New York in November and December respectively; Balanchine saw Brigitta at every available moment, showered her with expensive presents and repeatedly begged her to marry him. He seemed to be getting nowhere when, without warning, on Christmas Eve 1938, she said yes. He could hardly believe it, but they were married that very night after her performance, taking the ferry across to Staten Island where a judge was waiting for them. They returned to a party given by Brigitta's mother – a Christmas party which, when they broke the news, became a wedding party. On that night George believed himself to be the happiest man on earth.

Alas, there was the morning to be reckoned with – all mornings from now on. Temperamentally they were incompatible – the worst thing in marriage, said the playwright Frederick Lonsdale, who had experienced it. Balanchine was adoring, while Brigitta was fond but youthfully impatient. They remained husband and wife for seven years, which included many separations and attempts at reconciliation. Brigitta speaks of several reasons for the failure of the marriage: the thirteen years between them, her own immaturity and George's maturity which she describes as 'calmness and gentleness', and, of course, the perpetual physical separations caused by their work. Listening to her, I was struck by two things – calmness and gentleness, though wonderful in middle age were surely not the qualities most wanted by a successful beauty in her early twenties, and the pursuit of ambition which – though never mentioned – seemed to be the strongest force for them both. Certainly she was ambitious, understandably when she had the musical comedy world at her feet, and she possessed a strong determined mother who was closely involved in her daughter's career – reminiscent of both Tamara Toumanova and Margot Fonteyn. George always put his work first. The sadness lay in the divergence of their respective ambitions.

Many tales are told of Balanchine's misery during this period of his life – some, I think, lurid and overblown. But there is no doubt that he was deeply unhappy, both personally and professionally. With Brigitta he filmed *On Your Toes* at the Warner Brothers studios, but this was to be one of the last of his commercial successes. His money was fast disappearing and, after a couple of Broadway flops, it had gone. More than once he was forced to borrow from friends. He longed to be working with a ballet company again; the school flourished and he was teaching regularly, but he desperately missed the business of invention and creation.

Towards the end of 1939 he received a final slap in the face. A new American company was formed – Ballet Theater – with backing from the millionairess Lucia Chase. Great public interest and enthusiasm were expressed, and eleven American and European choreographers were invited to contribute ballets for the new company. George Balanchine's name was not among them. If there was one thing he didn't need at this moment it was humiliation, and that it should come from the source where his heart lay made it even worse.

His fortunes could not have been lower. Lincoln Kirstein was dismayed, thinking him 'lost to the ballet' and lost as a man, and Balanchine knew he was losing a wife whom he worshipped. It was a tragedy because, probably for the only time in his life, he had been swept away by his emotions. He had dropped every defence – the detachment and self-sufficiency, the enforced and preferred loneliness – and bared himself completely to another human being. To find himself rejected while in this pathetically vulnerable state was a wound from which, in my opinion, he never recovered. His later life and relationships were coloured indelibly by the experience.

He and Brigitta always remained friends and met regularly both socially and professionally. She is loyalty itself when speaking of him, and full of admiration for his achievements. She later married Goddard Lieberson, head of Columbia Broadcasting, had two sons and shared a happy life with him until his recent death. She still lives in their large apartment, with a stunning view over the East River. Fascinating in conversation, she has interesting and revealing things to say, not least about her years with George. But I remember best a story told to me by another remarkable woman, Barbara Horgan, who was secretary and personal assistant to Balanchine for many years. In 1968 she took Balanchine to stay with her mother in Taos, New Mexico, for a short holiday. The telephone rang – it was Brigitta in Santa Fe where she was appearing in Stravinsky's lyric drama *Perséphone*. Mrs Horgan had never before met Brigitta though she had a slight acquaintance with Balanchine's third wife, Maria Tallchief, and a fondness for his fourth, Tanaquil LeClercq, whom she knew well. During an evening at the opera house in Santa Fe Mrs Horgan found herself alone with George and said to him, 'Mr Balanchine, I know it's none of my business, but I think the woman who really means most to you is Mrs Lieberson.' He nodded, slowly and seriously, and answered, 'Yes – oh yes.'

15
Finding the Way

In 1940 the Second World War was gripping Europe, but in America life continued normally enough. George arranged dances for Brigitta in a film for 20th Century Fox called *I Was an Adventuress*, and then involved himself whole-heartedly in an unusual all-black Broadway musical comedy, *Cabin in the Sky*, which starred the unforgettable Ethel Waters. He cared deeply about the success of this show, putting his last savings into it and staging the entire production himself. The ballets he arranged for Katherine Dunham and her dancers were particularly brilliant. The musical was hailed as a triumph by the tough New York critics and the public loved it, but curiously it made no money. As life began to drain from the show George did everything he could to save it, finally contacting Goldwyn in Hollywood. But wily Sam wouldn't take the risk and the show died.

In early 1941 a company calling itself the Original Ballets Russes appeared at the 51st Street Theater in New York. 'Original' was a quaint word to use, but there were many old friends among its members, including Toumanova and Roman Jasinsky. Asked if he would create a new work for them, George needed no second invitation. He chose Stravinsky's Violin Concerto in D – the composer himself came to conduct – and the ballet was *Balustrade*, one of the first completely abstract ballets that he wrote. Exactly three performances were given and the critics screamed their disapproval in unison. John

Martin wrote, perhaps somewhat colourfully, that 'gifted American artists are starving' while 'there is money available for the production of European importations of this calibre'. Even so, Balanchine was happy; he had enjoyed every minute of his work, he loved and admired his principal dancers, and Stravinsky had been delighted, saying that it was 'one of the most satisfactory visualisations of any of my theater works'.

Lincoln Kirstein was also pleased by the turn of events. During the preceding years he had been quietly sponsoring a small group of dancers – Ballet Caravan – and now he saw a chance to involve George in their work. Fate came to his aid when Nelson Rockefeller was appointed to the State Department as a co-ordinator in Latin American affairs. As an initial gesture of cultural goodwill he suggested a tour by an American theatre company. It was the ideal opportunity, and with government, Rockefeller and Kirstein backing Balanchine and Ballet Caravan set off for Rio de Janeiro. The small group was enhanced by several members of the old American Ballet, William Dollar and Lew Christensen among them.

The tour opened on 25 June. The repertoire included *Serenade*, now sophisticated and streamlined, *Apollo* with Christensen as the god, and two new ballets of distinction, *Ballet Imperial* and *Concerto Barocco*, to Bach's Double Violin Concerto in D Minor. Balanchine's inspiration for these works seems, in many ways, an unlikely one. Marie-Jeanne, the first ballerina to emerge from the School of American Ballet, was of French-Italian parentage and Lincoln Kirstein had nurtured her development with the Caravan group. A slightly rough diamond, she appears slim and svelte in some photographs of the time, then chunky and muscular in others. In neither guise does she look the type of dancer to attract Balanchine, but her fantastic technique led him to create rôles of the highest virtuosity for her. Both ballets were without story, simply a visual expression of music, and they are two of his finest in this genre.

They were away for four months, then returned to New York where the dancers had to disband and George found himself back in the commercial theatre. The tour had been only a moderate success, but he had proved to himself that he could

still make marvellous ballets. This knowledge helped him
through a couple of easily forgotten Broadway shows and into
two operettas – *Rosalinda* and *The Merry Widow* – and a new
hit show, *Song of Norway*; all were enjoyable, lucrative, and
successful with the public.

At this time he took on one further assignment, an offer
which might have daunted many choreographers – he was
invited by the Ringling Brothers Circus to arrange a dance
number for fifty young elephants! He agreed, telephoned Stravinsky in California, and together they chose a Polka; the music
was composed and mailed and George started rehearsals with
these exceptional *danseuses*. Each elephant wore a tutu, a
pretty head-dress and ear-rings; fifty starlets of the circus were
perched on their backs, with Brigitta in the centre on the star
elephant, Modoc. The choreography was simple but effective,
and the public who came to the performances at Madison
Square Gardens were greatly amused. The elephants, however,
were not ecstatic about Stravinsky's music and flapped their
ears vigorously whenever the band struck up.

Connie Clausen, now a distinguished New York literary
agent, was one of the starlets and she later wrote her memoirs of
circus life, entitled *I Love You, Honey, But the Season's Over*.
She describes, with gratitude, Balanchine's arrival in Florida
for rehearsals at the circus headquarters. His quiet courtesy
made such a contrast to the tough, cynical manners of the
trainers that, as she writes. 'We'd have walked into a cage full of
hungry lions for him.' This was one of George's greatest
strengths: he had made the same impact in the musical comedy
theatre, where chorus dancers found a new liberation in working with him. Accustomed to rough and ready treatment, often
spiked with sarcasm, from managers and directors, they saw
Balanchine as a saviour, and danced for him as for no one else.

Meanwhile Balanchine's school, still in its dusty old pre-
mises, was now well established. In the early 1940s scholar-
ships were awarded, one of which was given to a long-legged
girl of eleven, Tanaquil LeClercq, and others to two talented
boys, Jacques d'Amboise, also eleven, and Edward Villella,
aged ten. By the mid-1940s there were two hundred pupils all
learning to dance in the loose-limbed, neo-classic style which

was Balanchine's trademark. It was a wonderful foundation for
his future company.

George now received an invitation from another ballet company, this time in the capacity of rescuer. Members of the old
Ballets Russes de Monte Carlo, with some American dancers,
had been touring the United States, still using the old name but
with sadly slipping standards. Serge Denham, the impresario
presenting them, was worried enough to call Balanchine and
beg for help in 'pulling it all together'. As a result, from 1944 to
1946 George did just that: he was ruthless in dismissing *passé*
Russians and bringing in younger, fresher Americans, drilling
the dancers to a higher level of technical excellence and adding
five new ballets to their repertoire. Shura Danilova, who led the
company, formed a partnership with a charming and talented
Englishman, Frederic Franklin. They danced together for many
years, coming as guest stars to our company at Covent Garden
in 1948. One evening, when Shura had injured her foot, I was
her last-minute replacement as Swanhilda in *Coppélia*, a part I
had danced many times. Freddie Franklin was an exceptional
partner – strong, easy, unfussed – and it was one of the happiest
performances I ever took part in.

The rejuvenated Monte Carlo troupe included many gifted
young dancers some of whom would become famous with the
New York City Ballet when that pipe-dream for Balanchine and
Kirstein finally became reality. Among them were Ruthanna
Boris, who also had choreographic talent, Mary Ellen Moylan,
the best of all interpreters of *Ballet Imperial*, Nicholas
Magallanes, and a young potential ballerina, Maria Tallchief.
Her parentage was fascinating, an Osage Indian father and a
Scottish-Irish-Dutch mother, a mixture which produced a strik-
ing appearance allied to a tremendous talent. From their first
meeting George was much taken with her.

He was also caught up with many other commitments. After
two more Broadway shows, choreography for several New
Opera Company productions and another film, *Star-spangled
Rhythm*, he was at last invited to create a ballet for Ballet
Theater. *Waltz Academy*, with a score by his old Diaghilev
friend, Vittorio Rieti, was the choice. Next he created a ballet for
a company calling itself Ballet International, with décor and

costumes by another friend, Salvador Dali, and with Eglevsky
as principal dancer; choreography for Brigitta as Ariel in a New
York production of Shakespeare's *The Tempest*; then off to
Mexico City with Marie-Jeanne, William Dollar and twelve
American Ballet members, where he arranged dances for three
operas and presented three of his own works, together with
Fokine's *Les Sylphides* in a staging by Dollar. After that he
returned to New York for a musical show at the Century
Theater, *Mr Strauss Goes to Boston*. George was a man who
couldn't say no.

On 22 January 1946 a strange and, in retrospect, ghoulish
episode took place. The setting was the Waldorf-Astoria Hotel
and the occasion a benefit for the March of Dimes to raise
money for polio research. Balanchine arranged a short ballet for
students from the school, with Tanaquil LeClercq, now fifteen,
as its centrepiece. The brief scenario concerned an Academy of
Dance with young pupils happily leaping and spinning. Enter a
black-clad figure, the Threat of Polio, Balanchine himself, who
touches the central girl and she falls paralysed to the ground. A
wheelchair is brought and she is placed in it, 'dancing'
touchingly with her arms and hands; then, after a shower of
silver rain, she leaps from her chair, restored to health and
vitality. It was an understandable theme for Balanchine to have
chosen for such an occasion, but his choice of the two leading
players was to be a haunting memory in the years ahead.

As the months of 1946 passed two matters were uppermost in
his mind. The first concerned Lincoln Kirstein, who had
returned from three years in the Monuments and Fine Arts
section of the US Army with a further inheritance, which he
planned to use for a completely new artistic venture. His ideas
coincided exactly with Balanchine's, as both men were disenchanted with the commercialism of the New York theatre.
Surely there were better ways to present the ballet to the
public? Gradually their ideas began to take shape.

George's second preoccupation was Maria Tallchief. Not only
had his admiration for her work been growing steadily, but he
had discovered a special bond with her, not shared by any other
dancer. She was also a pianist. Indeed, she must have been a
remarkable child, for her ballet training in California with

Nijinsky's sister, Bronislava, went hand in hand with musical studies to such effect that, at the age of twelve, she gave a recital – playing Chopin's E Minor Piano Concerto in the first half and dancing in the second half. I cannot think of any other dancer with two such developed talents except Carlotta Grisi, the original Giselle in 1841, who had such a lovely singing voice that she had great difficulty in deciding which career to follow. And the similarity goes further; Carlotta's sister, Teresa, became a celebrated opera singer, while Maria's sister, Marjorie, shares her striking appearance and great talent as a dancer.

Maria married Balanchine in August 1946. She was twenty-one, he was forty-two, and it lasted for five years. Like Brigitta, she speaks of him today with complete loyalty, admiration and feeling. But there is one great difference – she speaks of him as a teacher and balletmaster, not as a husband. There is reverence in every word, and love, certainly – but not, I think, the kind of love that one expects to hear from a wife about a former husband. Balanchine's years with and without Brigitta had completed the deadening process begun in his childhood, and he now formed relationships based on work, and work alone. He had lost none of his humour and prankishness, he adored cooking and relaxing with friends – Russians again in the ascendency – but he kept his defences intact. He never again fell in love with a woman just for herself.

The ideas and plans he worked on with Lincoln Kirstein were extremely select. To avoid all contact with hectic commercial enterprises they decided to form a group called Ballet Society. Their public would be subscription only; everything presented would be new and experimental, covering modern dance as well as the ballet; there would be performances of small chamber operas such as Gian-Carlo Menotti's *The Medium* and *The Telephone*, and the scheme even envisaged books on the dance and dance films.

Balanchine had many students available in his school and from the old American Ballet, and several members of the Monte Carlo and Ballet Theater companies came to work with him. There was only one problem – where to present the performances. Finally a hall was chosen, the auditorium of a

building with an unlikely name – the Central High School of
Needle Trades. It had all the amateur quality of a village hall: no
proper stage, simply a raised platform with a curtain; hard,
uncomfortable chairs; the orchestra on the same level as the
audience and the conductor higher still, so that even with
craned necks the public could see very little. And the décor was
terrible. It is difficult to imagine a more doom-laden setting, but
George was his usual equable self and filled with enthusiasm
and invention. The opening night was scheduled for 20 November 1946, and he had high hopes for the two new works he
would present.

He had gone back to Maurice Ravel, whom he had treated so
flippantly in his youthful Diaghilev days, and to the same score,
L'Enfant et les Sortilèges, in which he now found abundant and
subtle treasure. This lyric fantasy would be the first half of the
programme, the singers unseen in the wings. For the second
half he would play a trump card, a ballet called *The Four
Temperaments* with a score by Paul Hindemith written to his
own commission some years earlier – a time when he was
making so much money on Broadway that he was at a loss to
know how to spend it. He had written to Hindemith asking the
price of a Theme and Four Variations for piano and string
orchestra, and had received the welcome reply of five hundred
dollars. As the composition progressed, George gathered Russian musician friends in his apartment to play the music as it
came through the post. These occasions must have been rare
indeed – one of the violinists was the superb Nathan Milstein.

The opening night arrived, bringing a large audience to the
hard chairs of the School of Needle Trades. It was a curious
moment for a few New York critics who, not being subscription
members, had to creep in and hope to find a chair, their faces
flushed with unaccustomed embarrassment. The orchestra
entered and took their places. There was the usual tuning up,
general anticipation, and then – nothing. Nothing, that is,
except banging and hammering from behind the curtain and a
great deal of instrumental practice by the musicians in front of
it. This went on for a full half hour. There is no more dreadful
prelude to a performance – dancers become edgy and nervous,
and many audiences start the uncomfortable slow handclap,

which has a terrible tumbril sound from the other side of the curtain; a Broadway audience would certainly have walked out. But the subscribers were more tolerant and undoubtedly curious, and they stayed. The curtain parted and, in the words of the critic and ballet historian Anatole Chujoy, 'There was magic on the stage.'

It was an evening of surprise and exhilaration, by no means perfect in presentation but demonstrating a notable development in Balanchine's choreographic style. I feel that he was free, for the first time in America, of the wish to please. I think that his years in the commercial theatre had taught him the full value of his own ideals and ambitions, and he was indeed fortunate in the belief and backing of Lincoln Kirstein.

In the Ravel and Hindemith ballets he made no concession to anyone or anything. He merged modern and classical movement in a mélange of his own; he used stillness, then dramatic physical pyrotechnics, exactly as the music suggested, regardless of tradition or fashion. He did so with confidence and daring, which always brings an admiring response from the public. But, better still, it brought recognition of his courage and maturity – and in these matters the public is rarely wrong.

16
City Center

Ballet Society gave only three performances in the School of Needle Trades during the winter of 1946–7. They were enjoyed and much admired, yet a large question mark seemed to hang over the whole enterprise – what was Balanchine up to? The lack of commercialism proved puzzling to those who felt it was too rarefied to be healthy. Even Lincoln Kirstein, though never doubting his belief in the manner of presentation, watched dolefully as his money was eaten away by each new production. Temperamentally he was prone to troughs of depression, anticipating disaster long before it struck, and whether George's perennial optimism was a help or an irritant it is impossible to know.

Typically, Balanchine didn't have all his choreographic eggs in Ballet Society's basket. In early 1947 he arranged dances for Mary Ellen Moylan and a young Mexican, Francisco Moncion – both now with Ballet Society – in a production of the operetta *The Chocolate Soldier*, presented at the New Century Theater in New York. He was with them for the February previews, but sailed for Europe with Maria before the opening night. He had accepted an invitation from the Paris Opéra to be guest ballet-master and choreographer for several months. The Opéra was going through a difficult post-war time and, not surprisingly, the main source of trouble was again M. Serge Lifar.

The present trouble concerned wartime collaboration with the Germans. Even today there is still dissension about this among theatre people who lived through the war in occupied countries. Collaborators said that their own countrymen would have been deprived of all entertainment had they not worked for the enemy. Others, adamant in their refusal to co-operate, went underground and survived by other means. One of the most uncompromising was the celebrated French actress, Françoise Rosay, who would not even speak to a German. I remember an embarrassing day when she visited the *Red Shoes* set in England in 1947: our leading actor, Anton Walbrook (born Adolph Walbrüch) waited for her arrival with unconcealed excitement, telling us of their great pre-war friendship. As she walked into the studio, Anton advanced with outstretched arms; she walked straight past him as if he didn't exist, without even a flicker of a glance in his direction. Anton was in fact Austrian, but, as she would have been the first to point out, so was Hitler.

As a collaborator Lifar had done well for himself. After the Liberation, despite the frequent sight of shaven heads and public humiliation for others throughout France, Lifar remained untouched; but only for a time. French opinion was too strong, so the Opéra dismissed him and in his place invited a succession of guest balletmasters from abroad. George came back to Europe and to the great opera house which had failed him in the past. It was to fail him again.

The visit began well enough: *Serenade*, *Apollo* and *Baiser de la Fée* were welcomed with success and much public interest. Toumanova was leading the company – her personal success was assured – and young Maria, the first American dancer at the Opéra since 1839, was considered more than promising in the Stravinsky ballets. Balanchine's contract specified one new work, and for this he chose Bizet's happy and tuneful First Symphony, written when the composer was barely seventeen. The ballet's original title was *Le Palais de Crystal*, but this was later changed to the simpler *Symphony in C*. All the youthful freshness of the music was caught by Balanchine in his choreography – it is one of his most joyful ballets and remains a favourite with audiences of all nationalities. Even the fastidious Parisians, when it was brand-new and unknown, were beguiled.

Behind the scenes it was not so rosy. The Opéra dancers, accustomed to the flattery of Lifar, thought Balanchine a cold fish. Good technical dancing he took for granted, and any praise given was perfunctory to the point of curtness. The company already contained a strong faction in favour of Lifar's rehabilitation; the brisk manner in which George conducted his rehearsals fanned this feeling, and soon a petition with many signatures arrived on the desk of the Minister of Arts. It called for 'no guests, no foreigners', and the welcome appointment of a well-tried, permanent balletmaster. Lifar was virtually on his way back.

Balanchine's second and final departure from Paris was similar to his first in 1929. Though his status with the Opéra was that of a guest, he had started to think that, as a permanent post, it might be the answer to the uncertainty of Ballet Society in New York. Could he not shuttle to and fro – and could not the stability of Paris make possible the experimentation he wanted in America? He was now an American citizen and glad to be, but he was a European to his fingertips and, fleetingly, he saw his future there. Lifar's imminent, triumphant return to his adoring company was the decisive factor. George and Maria sailed for home with feelings of depression and failure.

But, stimulated as always by New York, Balanchine was soon hard at work on two ballets: Mozart for Ballet Society and Tchaikovsky for Ballet Theater. The Mozart *Symphonie Concertante* was skeletal in its sparseness and simplicity and pleased neither public nor critics. Maria admired it greatly but gave a dancer's view of the choreography: 'It was like taking your medicine every day.' The Tchaikovsky *Theme and Variations* had a different reception, as nearly ecstatic as anyone could have wished. Leading the cast was a superb Cuban dancer, Alicia Alonso, partnered by a great 'gentleman' of the ballet, Igor Youskevitch; also in the original cast was a name that would later be long associated with Balanchine ballets – Melissa Hayden. The only sour note came from Lincoln Kirstein, who thought the ballet less than the choreographer's best. He was a little peeved that Lucia Chase's company should be reaping such success and, in the manner of Diaghilev, he found universal acclaim suspect. It was an odd, perverse streak in his nature.

Nevertheless, it gave him great pleasure to see George, now forty-three, recognized at last as a master of his art, and *Theme and Variations* may well have been the turning point in Balanchine's American career.

Typically, George wasted no time basking in public adulation but was soon at work on his next production. This was to be a new *Orpheus* with a score by Stravinsky, a ballet devised in the style of a seventeenth-century opera. Though they were old colleagues, this was the first time they had worked together from the very beginning of a new theme. They were perfectly matched, their respective ideas dovetailing smoothly, and the work was exciting and satisfying for them both. During the early discussions, before any music had been composed, Balanchine learnt a valuable lesson from Stravinsky. The composer asked him how much music he would like for the central pas de deux for Orpheus and Eurydice, 'Oh, about two and a half minutes,' was Balanchine's reply.

The retort came quickly: 'Don't say "about". There is no such thing as "about". Is it two minutes, two minutes and fifteen seconds, two minutes and thirty seconds or something in between? Give me the exact time, please, and I'll come as close to it as possible.' How different from poor Tchaikovsky, who had wrestled with Petipa's cuts of 'twelve bars here' and demands for an additional 'twenty-four bars there', a task he never mastered with ease.

The first choice of designer was Pavel Tchelitchev, but he had grown increasingly eccentric and dominant over the years and after several difficult weeks he withdrew from the production. Kirstein suggested instead the Japanese artist, Isamu Noguchi. His ideas were much more in tune with the general conception and Balanchine was delighted by his feeling for light and space. The score was completed, the choreography arranged – Stravinsky at Balanchine's elbow as he would be the conductor – and the opening performance was scheduled for 28 April 1948.

There enters now a woman who should be given more recognition than she has ever received – the business manager of Ballet Society, Frances Hawkins. She had been negotiating with the New York City Center of Music and Drama for the use of the Center on West 55th Street for the *Orpheus* première, and she had – with difficulty – persuaded Lincoln Kirstein to schedule three further performances for the general public. It was the most far-sighted move she could possibly have made. In many ways, the creation of the New York City Ballet stems from this decision by Frances Hawkins.

On 28 April the subscription public watched a beautiful and extraordinary ballet with principal performances from Nicholas Magallanes, a noble Orpheus, Maria Tallchief, a lyrical Eurydice, and Tanaquil LeClercq, a brilliant and ferocious Bacchante. Setting, costumes and effects, music and dance, all blended together as if they could not have been otherwise. Whatever the personal preference of individual members of the audience, there was one constant factor for everyone – the ballet seemed complete and inevitable in its conception and execution. The public and critical response was good; in Edwin Denby's case, overwhelming – he remained 'too moved' to leave his seat during the interval. This did not go unnoticed.

At one of the subsequent public performances a man called Morton Baum joined the audience. He was a tax lawyer and not the least interested in the ballet, but as he was chairman of the City Center finance committee he thought he should see what was going on. Expecting an indifferent, possibly boring evening, he was quite unprepared for his feelings of excitement as he watched the stage. By the last fall of the curtain he had become a Balanchine addict – he had seen *Orpheus*, *Symphonie Concertante* and *Symphony in C* – and was determined to put Ballet Society under contract to City Center.

He had an uphill task with his tough finance committee: one of its members was Gerald Warburg, Edward's brother, who told him, 'You play around with Balanchine and Kirstein and you'll lose your shirt.' Gradually Baum talked them all round. Then he approached Kirstein, who was amazed and thankful, as his own money was at its last gasp; he talked to George, who knew this would be salvation; and only then did Baum go back to his desk to work out how on earth he was going to finance this company. The situation is reminiscent of Gabriel Astruc and Diaghilev before the first 1909 season of the Ballets Russes.

The City Center of Music and Drama is a dreadful building. A former Mecca Temple decorated in bogus oriental style, the city acquired it in 1941 from a faternal lodge who hadn't paid their taxes. It was converted into a centre for music and drama at popular prices but the stage was small with the minimum of wing space, the dressing rooms were cramped, and the orchestra pit reminded Stravinsky of a men's lavatory. But it was a theatre. This would now be the company's official home and, when the first season opened in the autumn of that year, Balanchine's dancers had a new name – the New York City Ballet.

The company is now so celebrated, so established, that it is hard to imagine the first years at City Center. There are many people who consider 1948 to 1964 in this old, ugly theatre to have been Balanchine's most brilliantly inventive period. Certainly at forty-four he was in his prime, and the fact of having a theatre and a settled company gave him a tremendous fillip. The ballet world reacted favourably and many dancers from other companies came to join him – Melissa Hayden, Janet Reed, Diana Adams, Nora Kaye, Hugh Laing, Eglevsky and, most notably, Jerome Robbins. Robbins was an excellent dancer and an even better choreographer, though still in the early stages of his career. Balanchine admired his talents, gave him opportunities and much encouragement, and made him associate artistic director in 1949. This is more unusual than it may appear: I remember dancers with the Royal Ballet who hoped for choreographic experience but, being denied it, left for European companies where they received subsequent and deserved acclaim. When I hear denigration of Balanchine for lack of generosity towards other choreographers, as I frequently do, I wish his partnership with Jerome Robbins could be remembered. Robbins made an appreciative comment to Bernard Taper about the influence of Balanchine: 'He made me see that the work was more important than the success . . . that work in progress was what mattered most.'

Morton Baum's recipe for a solvent company was exactly the same as Diaghilev's so many years before – opera ballets. The New York City Opera, based at the Center, was now given a new lease of life with imaginative dances from George and elegant performances from his dancers. *Carmen* was closely followed by *The Marriage of Figaro*, *La Traviata*, *Don Giovanni*, *Aïda*, and a happy choice for a Russian, *Eugene Onegin*. Simultaneously, Balanchine was whirling through the streets to the St James Theater to arrange five numbers for Frank Loesser's musical *Where's Charley?*, with the ebullient Ray Bolger triumphant in the title role. He was also restaging *Concerto Barocco* from Ballet Caravan days for his own company and, as a little *bonne bouche*, he was directing Jean Giraudoux's play *The Madwoman of Chaillot* at the Belasco Theater, starring the splendid Martita Hunt from England. All this took place between 10 October and 27 December – it makes one breathless, and also doubtful about any possibility of domestic life with Maria.

So it continued in 1949 – new ballets, revivals, opera ballets and the odd pas de deux here and there. The most important venture was his own version of the hallowed Fokine–Stravinsky ballet *The Firebird*. This was a daring move, taken with the blessing of Stravinsky but with dismay from the more traditionally minded audiences. The highly coloured décor and costumes, reminiscent of a child's book of fairy tales, were by Marc Chagall and, in place of Fokine's mime drama, Balanchine substituted dancing. Everyone danced in his *Firebird*, and this seems to have been the pill which the traditionalists were unable to swallow – odd, I think, in a ballet. The reception in New York was good, and Maria made a glittering impression in the central rôle; it was one of her greatest successes, wherever the ballet was performed. Her strange, handsome cast of features had a compelling, mysterious quality which, for me, enhanced her interpretation still further. But the ballet was given a rough ride on many occasions, particularly in London which so often displays a slavish adherence to tradition.

Balanchine was preparing this production as we, the Sadler's Wells company, were dancing at the old Metropolitan Opera House on the first British tour of America. Our success was phenomenal – too much, I think, for the quality of performance – but the Americans were seeing the Maryinsky classics in their original full-length versions for the first time and were overwhelmed. During our tour, plans were discussed for a New York City Ballet season at Covent Garden in the following summer, and for Balanchine alone to visit us in the spring to stage a ballet. The possibility of a London season for his company must have pleased George greatly: foreign exposure for his young dancers was exactly what their steady development required.

17
Success and Tragedy

Balanchine arrived in London in early March 1950 and our company went into rehearsal for *Ballet Imperial*. George stayed with Frederick Ashton in his charming little house in Knightsbridge; unused to the damp English climate, he was always cold, and Fred remembers constant journeys to his room with rugs and electric fires. During these weeks Fred heard no mention of the company or of the progress of rehearsals. The only indication of work on the ballet were the sounds of George playing passages from the Tchaikovsky second concerto on Fred's piano before leaving for the theatre.

They had first met in the late 1920s, and again in 1933 when Balanchine was in London at the Savoy Theatre. They were almost exact contemporaries – Lifar and Dolin too – and, as Ninette de Valois drily put it, 'Oh, there was a lot of jealousy there, dear – a *lot*.' When I talked to Fred about Balanchine he described his initial 'awe' and how, after the Diaghilev years, 'he had so much more behind him than I had'. He thought him a very good-looking man, with 'a very fine Georgian face', and here Fred stroked his own long nose in a gesture suggesting delicacy. He was full of admiration for the early ballets shown at the Savoy, though *Cotillon* and *Concurrence* were always his favourites – but for George himself at this time a little criticism crept in: 'We called him "The Voice" because he always did all the talking – no one else ever got a word in.' Much of the talking seems to have been about food and wine and delicious cookery, which bored Fred dreadfully; he is no cook, and for conversation prefers a diet of gossip and anecdote, like many of his theatrical generation. Perhaps this bored George equally? I asked Fred if he had ever sampled Balanchine's cooking and he said, 'No – he often talked of me coming to dine but never actually invited me.' In fact, Balanchine seems to have been extremely lax about returning hospitality; Fred twice travelled to New York to make ballets for the City company and said that he had never received any personal invitation on either visit.

Speaking of their shared profession, Fred became increasingly critical of Balanchine's development. Stravinsky, he thought, was the culprit, influencing George into a spare and soulless visual conception similar to the composer's spare and sometimes arid music. He praised a few of his pure dance ballets for their quality of invention, but always ended with his view of a gifted choreographer who had lost his way and whose work had become unemotional and heartless. Fred had not enjoyed working on his own *Illuminations* ballet with the City company, though he greatly admired the dancers, speaking of their 'vitality and athleticism'. But he felt that George had been less than co-operative: he often made dancers unavailable for rehearsals, and himself left for Italy on the day of Fred's première. Listening to Ashton on Balanchine was, to my ears, like listening to Mark Antony's famous speech of denigration, then eulogy, in *Julius Caesar* – but in reverse.

Ballet Imperial was a success. Balanchine lifted us all to high technical achievement and we felt a great sense of occasion in the production. Beryl Grey was deservedly admired; her long, fluid line was ideal for Balanchine choreography, though she herself felt, as she says, 'very below par' at this time, having just recovered from jaundice. In spite of this, I cannot imagine that her performance could have been improved. The previous year, in New York, she had attended several classes at the School of American Ballet and had been intimidated, first by Balanchine and his style of teaching, and then by the virtuosity of the dancers all round her. 'Their technique!' she exclaimed. 'Their fantastically high développés!', and she had come away deeply impressed. There is no doubt that Balanchine's teaching was on a different level from anything in Europe at this time.

George returned to New York, his company and Maria. Their proposed Covent Garden season in the summer was now definite and our administrator, David Webster, had told Frances Hawkins, 'Covent Garden will make the New York City Ballet.' This was a somewhat arrogant statement from a man whose own ballet company, had, in a sense, been made by America the previous year. In July and August London was given its first sight of eighteen ballets, twelve by Balanchine, of which three were 'story' ballets -- *Firebird*, *Orpheus* and *Prodigal Son* – and another with a definite theme was *Jones Beach*, which he arranged in collaboration with Jerome Robbins. The music for this was by Juriaan Andriessen, the bathing suits by Jantzen, and the four movements were divertingly entitled 'Sunday', 'Rescue from Drowning', 'War with Mosquitoes', and 'Hot Dogs'. The repertoire included works by Lew Christensen, Todd Bolender, William Dollar, and two by Robbins, *The Guests* and *Age of Anxiety*, as well as Frederick Ashton's *Illuminations* and the first performance of *The Witch* by our young British/South African Dancer John Cranko.

Their reception was mixed, with many enthusiastic audiences and many critical brickbats. The two ballets treated most harshly were *Firebird* and Ashton's *Illuminations*, of which the *Dancing Times* wrote, 'It can only be comprehensible to those with the inclination to study the sordid existence, unhealthy mind and more frantic poems of a decadent, nineteenth-century poet, Arthur Rimbaud.' *Firebird* was given a tremendous drubbing by every critic except the perceptive Richard Buckle of the *Observer*. There were no doubts in his mind: 'One thing that is clear about Balanchine's *Firebird* which some of my matronly colleagues have been deploring, is that it is a great deal better than Fokine's. Fokine's had atmosphere, agreed, but so has Victoria Station. Balanchine's *Firebird* is an exciting ballet with dancing in it.'

This is enjoyable criticism, witty, infor⁻ ative, and unhampered by tiresome technicalities. And Buckle had another *bon mot* for the company, writing that 'a memorial should be erected to all the gallant Americans who fell at Covent Garden'. This was a reference to the appalling old stage, from which we had suffered since the post-war reopening of the Opera House in 1946. The Americans had been going down like ninepins, unaware of the hazards. There was one monstrous section of stage, about two-thirds towards the footlights, which we had named 'Becher's Brook' after the most dangerous jump on the Aintree Grand National racecourse. Over the years we had become crafty, but if you were hopping along on one 'pointe' – as in Giselle's Act I solo – well, bad luck.

The final impression at the end of the season was of breathtaking classical dancing, athletic rather than poetic, but too many 'plotless' ballets for the public taste. July and August can be difficult months in the theatre, and the company found their audiences thinning away as people left London for their summer holidays. Back in New York, Balanchine, Kirstein and Morton Baum discovered a much bigger deficit than had been expected, and spirits were low – particularly low for Maria and George, who were thinking of separation. He even had thoughts at this time of leaving for Italy and the La Scala company of Milan. It would have been one disaster that Lincoln Kirstein had not anticipated.

The marriage to Maria had been no more successful than those to her predecessors, and like them it was she who wanted to end it. In later years Balanchine would sometimes stress that he had never left a wife, but that they had always left him – what a strange thing for a man to wish the world to know. Because of his frequent marriages he has been described as a Don Juan – but do Don Juans get married? Surely the whole point of a real Don Juan is that he never ties himself down? In many ways I think that Balanchine was the opposite of this famous womaniser.

One aspect of his personal life which has always puzzled me also seems to puzzle many of his close associates – the exceptional loyalty of the ex-wives, which never wavers, and the extraordinary ease with which they have always met and worked together. Was there, perhaps, a minimum of sex in these marriages? Sexual jealousy can be such a strong force in women, yet one never senses the slightest breath of such feelings among the women he loved. His marriage to Maria was annulled in 1952; in December that year he married Tanaquil

LeClercq and Maria continued her career as a ballerina of his company. It was a strange situation.

Tanaquil LeClercq was an authentic Balanchine product. She had been trained in his school from her earliest years, and her build, style and talents were exactly as he liked them. She also possessed an unexpected quality in a classicist – she could bring humour and wit to her dancing, and Balanchine used this with great effect in certain rôles which she created. From all accounts she was a funny, 'sparky' young woman – Maria speaks of 'a streak of craziness' in her – and George, with his own brand of quirky humour, must have found this an endearing trait.

After his return from London in the autumn of 1950 he had been as active as ever, staging fifteen productions before the end of 1951. There were revivals, a Pas de Deux, a Pas de Trois, four new ballets, his own version of Act II of *Swan Lake*, dances for Shakespeare's *Romeo and Juliet* and a musical comedy called *Courtin' Time*. There was also a Glinka Mazurka for four couples in which Balanchine danced, partnering Vida Brown. He made a comic caricature of himself in the traditional costume, 'ratty' teeth from the Imperial School days much in evidence.

Balanchine was in his element, with an established and increasingly successful company, a thriving school, and unlimited opportunity to let the flow of invention pour out of him. He used diverse music for diverse ballets – his favourite Mozart, Virgil Thomson, Mendelssohn, Hindemith, Riccardo Drigo, Delibes, Jean Françaix, Strauss the younger, Schoenberg, Charles Ives, and another American, Hershy Kay – all this and Tchaikovsky and Stravinsky too. No one can accuse Balanchine of not being sufficiently catholic in his choice of composers, and they provided endlessly varied springboards for his choreographic invention.

His nostalgia for Europe seems to have left him and he was completely in tune with America. His increasing use of American music and American themes was drolly reflected in his dress – checked shirts, pearl buttons, string ties and cowboy trousers and boots. Brigitta speaks of his 'terrible' taste in

clothes and how she 'tidied him up'. When I told her how
perfectly dressed (to my eyes, at least) he had appeared in
London, she at once answered, 'Yes – he was still under my
influence.'

In 1954, however, he returned to his European roots by
staging – contrary to existing City Ballet policy – a complete
Tchaikovsky ballet, The Nutcracker. In three acts, it is a full
evening's entertainment of nineteenth-century Russian charm
in which many children take part. The rehearsals for this ballet
must have been singularly nostalgic for Balanchine, for he had
vivid memories of the St Petersburg production, in which he
had had his first childhood success, and of many St Petersburg
institutions like the famous sweetstore, Yeliseyevsky's which
mirrored the second act of Tchaikovsky's ballet. At the age of
seventy-eight Balanchine described it to Solomon Volkov:
'Huge glass windows, rooms big enough for a palace, high
ceilings, opulent glass chandeliers, almost like the ones at the
Maryinsky. The floors at Yeliseyevsky's were covered in saw-
dust and you could not hear footsteps – it was like walking on
carpets. The store had sweets and fruits from all over the world
like in A Thousand and One Nights.' He stressed the element of
sugar and candy in all the second act characters of his Nutcracker, the Sugar Plum Fairy at the centre. Originally her
partner was Prince Coqueluche, presumably representing a
lozenge or cough drop as the French coqueluche means whoop-
ing cough! Balanchine wisely decided against preserving this
tradition, and the prince is now simply her Cavalier.

Balanchine was childless, but he had a special fondness for
children and a wonderful way with them. In his lifetime he
gave two generations of children the thrill and excitement of
their first stage experience in seasons of The Nutcracker. Over
the years this ballet has become the main moneyspinner for the
City Ballet and is staged by companies in many American
cities. A friend in New York told me recently that, for many
Americans, The Nutcracker simply is the New York City Ballet.

Another and more extensive European tour had been undertaken in 1952, consolidating the company's reputation abroad,
at home, and within itself. London was revisited, with similarly
mixed results; they went to Paris twice in the course of the tour,

to cities in Spain, Switzerland, the Netherlands, Germany, and
to Edinburgh for the Festival. In Barcelona, which gave the
Americans their greatest reception, there was a crescendo of
cheering, flowers rained down on the stage and doves were
released into the auditorium. For a performer there is no more
magical sound than that of the public in full cry, and it gave a
wonderful boost to company morale.

In 1956 they were again in Europe and, in October, arrived to
dance in Copenhagen. Touring is exhausting and many of the
dancers were feeling the strain, but Tanaquil LeClercq felt an
unusual tiredness and sickness. She danced *Swan Lake* at a
matinée performance and was scheduled to dance *Bourrée
Fantasque*, one of her witty rôles, at night. Speaking to John
Gruen for his book *The Private World of Ballet*, her friend and
colleague Patricia Wilde described that night:

> We used to do *Bourrée* interchangeably. On that same night I was
> doing *Pas de Dix*. When I finished, I went into the dressing room
> and asked her how she was feeling. She said that her back felt
> strange and she asked me to look at it. So I thought maybe she
> had a cold or something. I asked her if she wanted me to do
> *Bourrée* for her, but she said no, because she was already there
> and was made up. So she went out and danced it, and after that
> night she never walked again . . .

It was polio – the supreme tragedy for a brilliant dancer. She
was twenty-seven years old. Did she, as some people say, miss a
pre-tour inoculation because of incessant work? Had she, as
another says, leaned over the side of a boat in Venice earlier in
the tour and – perhaps for a dare? – drunk water from the canal?
No one could say, but this didn't prevent endless speculation.
Only one thing was clear – she was very ill and would possibly
be permanently paralysed from the waist down, so every
conceivable treatment must be found and tried. Balanchine was
distraught, never leaving his wife's hospital bedside, and he
had the support of her mother who had accompanied them on
the tour.

Ninette de Valois was also in Copenhagen and she speaks
touchingly of Balanchine's devotion, a side of him she hadn't

seen before. She was also struck by his intense medical interest – in the disease itself, its possible causes and the varied effects on different people, and in all the available treatments. She describes him as being 'just like a doctor'. He was already thinking of interesting and useful things to do from the restriction of a wheelchair, though always praying that this would not be necessary. But, tragically, it was. The little ballet he made for the March of Dimes Benefit when he, as Polio, touched the fifteen-year-old who fell paralysed, became a terrible and haunting memory.

18
Russia

Balanchine was absent from his company for almost a year.
When Tanaquil was able to leave the Copenhagen hospital he
took her to Warm Springs in Georgia – the American Georgia –
for further restorative treatment. Many people thought that his
career might be over and that he had lost all heart for the ballet,
and so it seemed during these months. But someone of Balanchine's creative genius cannot live without the constant use of
it. In the early autumn of 1957 he brought Tanaquil back to New
York, rejoined the company to find that standards of performance were not as they should be, and promptly set to work.

The enforced idleness had generated renewed energy and
powers of invention in the fifty-three-year-old choreographer,
and within ten weeks four new ballets were completed – one of
them a masterpiece. Markedly different in style, they included
Square Dance, an American form of dance with a real-life
'caller', Elisha C. Keeler, set to the music of Vivaldi (this, in the
language of Vivaldi's time, was a charming conceit); *Gounod
Symphony*, a symphonic work as its title suggests; and *Stars
and Stripes*, almost a parade ballet to the rousing marches of
Sousa, which Balanchine loved. This was dedicated to the
memory of the founder of the City Center and the much-loved
Mayor of New York, Fiorello (Little Flower) La Guardia – a
delightful name for this tough, spherical little man. The fourth
ballet, the undoubted masterpiece, was *Agon*, to a score
commissioned from Stravinsky. The music dedication was to

Kirstein and Balanchine, but perhaps should have included the Rockefeller Foundation which met the composer's not inconsiderable fee.

Any description of *Agon* can only give a faint flavour of the stage picture and movement. The setting was a pale blue cyclorama; the dancers wore black and white practice clothes, and there were no embellishments of any kind. *Agon* is the Greek for contest, and the dancers appeared in ever-changing groupings – eights, twelves, four couples, trios, four trios and yet more. They danced to music which was rhythmic, often staccato, and with that slightly acid quality of Stravinsky in his best vein. But it was the *way* in which they danced and the types of movement employed that made the ballet so exceptional.

Balanchine had imagined perfect, formal classical technique, laced here and there with modern movements and positions. The dancers gave the impression of dancing straight to the front, or at right-angles, facing each other, grouped in striking and unexpected ways. This was oddly satisfying, though I cannot explain why. One thought one had seen all this before, but in fact it was new and exciting and, at times, witty. The humour in many of the movements and held poses gave a feeling of freshness and youthfulness, as if the dancers were enjoying every minute of their contest.

In the centre of the ballet was a long and marvellous Pas de Deux, written for Diana Adams and Arthur Mitchell. This, too, was a type of contest, the technique used being highly complex and with hardly a lift in the entire duet. This was not only unusual, it was amazing. The two original dancers were as near-perfect as one could wish, and there was another element involved. Arthur Mitchell, a beautiful dancer with a great stage presence, is black – the first black classical dancer with the City Ballet. The stage picture formed by these two dancers – he in white shirt and black tights, Diana Adams, with white skin and black hair, also in black and white – is something I shall never forget.

The company was now making regular tours to the main American cities with increasing success, and in March 1958 came a stimulating tour to Japan, Australia and the Philippines.

Some ballet companies become stale with prolonged touring but the Americans seem to have reacted differently, becoming a more compact and confident unit with each foreign visit. New principals and soloists were emerging regularly, for Balanchine's sharp eyes noted every nuance of performance and enabled him to give younger dancers solo opportunities. One of the most interesting facets of his company was its lack of an old-fashioned corps de ballet. The body of his company possessed the technical calibre of soloists – this standard was expected, the training made it possible, and the ballets exploited it. The resulting excellence and often brilliance of ensemble dancing gave the company that particular 'look' which no other company achieved.

There was an important newcomer to City Center in 1958, not to the stage but to the orchestra pit. The English conductor from Covent Garden, Robert Irving, came to New York to replace Balanchine's long-resident conductor, Leon Barzin. He had met George in 1950 at the time of *Ballet Imperial*; then, in an emergency that summer, he had found himself conducting for the first American season in London, and today he speaks of his 'instant rapport' with Balanchine. By 1959 Bob Irving had been resident with the Covent Garden orchestra for ten years and was feeling the strain. In Toronto, on tour with the Royal Ballet, he received an invitation from Balanchine and flew south to meet him and Kirstein. His appointment as principal conductor was arranged immediately – as he says, 'It seemed a foregone conclusion on both sides.' He was in New York by late summer and his name appeared on City Center programmes in early September: a little older and a little larger, he is still the conductor for the City Ballet today.

Obviously happy and at home in America, he found his relationship with Balanchine 'always perfect, right to the end'. He has immense admiration for the company, describing it as 'in a different category altogether' from any other he has worked with. And he has particular fondness for certain dancers – Maria Tallchief is, I think, a special favourite. Unlike Fred Ashton, he received much private hospitality from Balanchine and remembers a farcical evening after a performance when he joined George and Tanaquil in their apartment. Dinner was to

be a Balanchine spaghetti and champagne. First the bottle
wouldn't open, and when it did, with a mini explosion, that
was the end of it. On to the spaghetti, which looked and smelt
delicious – but while straining it George was talking so ani-
matedly that he poured the lot down the sink.

The next three years passed in a welter of choreographic
activity. Seventeen productions were staged, most of them new,
but among them two revivals and dances for two Shakespeare
plays. He also wrote a solo – *The Warrior* – for André Eglevsky,
a unique dancer whom he tended to ignore. Sadly, he never
really liked Eglevsky's work – he thought his teaching superb
but not his dancing; and Maria speaks of this as prejudiced and
unperceptive, and I agree. But in his new ballets George's eye
was less fallible, though the more experimental works taxed the
public tolerance. He even made a foray into electronic music – a
ballet called *Electronics* – which was not at all to Bob Irving's
taste.

Martha Graham, the queen of modern dance, collaborated on
one production called *Episodes*. She and her dancers contributed Part I and Balanchine and his dancers Part II, the music
selected from the orchestral works of the uncompromising
Anton von Webern. It was a strange amalgam, the first part
showing Martha Graham's group in period costume, depicting
the death of Mary, Queen of Scots, and the second part showing
Balanchine at his most spare, angular and clinical. It was a
curiosity rather than a success and many critics felt that there
had been confusion somewhere along the line. I missed this
ballet and am not altogether sorry, as I have never yet been able
to share a room with the music of Webern.

A ballet I did see, and loved, was also from this period – the
Brahms *Liebeslieder Wälzer*. It too is divided into two parts.
The setting is a ballroom with four couples in evening dress
seated at little tables in trellised alcoves. In the first part there
are graceful, elegant variations on the waltz – varying pairs and
trios, grave and joyful, the white satin balldresses and soft
white evening slippers of the women creating a romantic
atmosphere. When the curtain rises on the second part, the
women are wearing *Sylphides* dresses and point shoes. The
dances become classically romantic and technical, virtuosity is

on display, and only at the end of the ballet do the couples reappear in their original costumes and positions at the little tables. Bernard Taper writes of a conversation with Balanchine after the opening performance, when the choreographer said, 'In the first act, it's the real people that are dancing. In the second act, it's their souls.' Presumably he meant to create a rarefied plane in the second part, far transcending the first, but for me this failed. The point shoe technicalities of his souls seemed dull and predictable after the unusual beauty and Brahmsian lyricism of his humans, and I would have been much happier to remain in that mood for the entire ballet.

The first six months of 1962 brought three new productions, a full-evening's *Midsummer Night's Dream* at City Center, dances and a full staging of *Eugen Onegin* at the Hamburg State Opera, and a dance-drama, *Noah and the Flood*, written specially for television in collaboration with Stravinsky. Balanchine was dissatisfied with his own contribution to *Noah* and was made miserable and angry by the commercialism of the television company, but his Mendelssohn *Dream* was a pleasure. It was his first original full-length ballet; somehow, with his mute dancers, he managed to convey all the complicated misunderstandings of Shakespeare's plot, and his choreography for the Fairy Kingdom, the Mortals and Rude Mechanicals was of great beauty. Late in August the company travelled to Europe, dancing in Germany and Austria during September en route for their most important European date – 9 October at Moscow's Bolshoi Theatre.

The six weeks that the Americans spent in Russia, dancing in five cities, were unforgettable and, for George, momentous and troubling. His love for his own country was strong, even if it was now only an idealistic love, for everywhere he saw the hand of the régime he hated. He had kept in touch with his family over the years, writing to his mother and at times of privation sending food parcels until these were eventually stopped by the authorities. His father had died in 1937, his mother only a few years before this visit, and his sister Tamara, who had become an architect and painter, had been killed in an air raid on Leningrad in the war. There was now only his younger brother, Andrey, and a much older half-brother.

Balanchine's spirits were low and he tried to concentrate exclusively on the company's performances.

The opening night in the Bolshoi was an occasion of supreme formality largely dictated by protocol. Ministers and ambassadors are not always the liveliest members of any gathering, and on this occasion the reception was a cool one. Balanchine had expected this, but was quite unprepared for the mounting excitement which greeted subsequent performances. They were given in the huge, modern Palace of Congresses in the Kremlin to audiences who stamped their feet and chorused Balanchine's name while he took curtain call after call. Different it may have been, but the Russians liked what they saw.

So the tour progressed, the critics critical and the public enthusiastic – even, to George's amazement, towards the stark Webern *Episodes* which had never won such success in New York. In Moscow, his daily company class was watched by many members of the Bolshoi Ballet and it must have been an emotional moment for him when the Russians held a reciprocal class – the teacher was old Pavel Gerdt's daughter, Andreyanov's widow, his own youthful favourite, Yelisaveta Gerdt.

In Leningrad his excitement grew as he visited all the landmarks of his childhood and adolescence. He had forgotten nothing but was sometimes saddened – the Cathedral of Our Lady of Kazan, where his father's music had been played and which had been the scene of his uncle's consecration, was now a silent museum. His frequent travelling companion was another Russian on the staff of the New York school, Mrs Nathalie Molostwoff. She observed his pleasure in the rediscovery of much of his past and in the ovations accorded to his company, and the mixed pleasure of meeting again many former student friends, some of whom had become good party men. But she was also aware of the strain. From the moment of his arrival in Russia Balanchine had been bombarded by interviews, requests to give talks to various groups, receptions when he would be expected to speak, and the semi-public classes. When the company left Leningrad for Kiev, he decided he could take no more and he boarded a plane back to New York.

A week later, calmer and steadier, he flew back, but this time

to Georgia. Performances were scheduled in Tbilisi and Baku
and hundreds of Georgians were greatly excited at the prospect
of welcoming the famous son of their 'Georgian Glinka'. His
week's rest had been well timed. He was fêted and mobbed, and
on the opening night, with too many seats occupied by party
officials, hordes of young Georgians stormed the theatre doors,
poured into the aisles and remained for an ecstatic performance. Balanchine's customary equanimity was broken and his
emotions were visible to everyone.

Then the receptions started, sometimes four in a day. Mrs
Molostwoff remembers how they stood, untasted drinks in their
hands, while interminable speeches were made, followed by a
banquet – then on to the next reception. She journeyed with
him 'overnight in a filthy train' to his father's original home in
Koutais; he visited his father's grave and met his half-brother, a
priest – one of the tiniest men he had ever seen. There were
many meetings with his own brother, Andrey, a composer like
their father and now married with three children. Andrey was
also rather small; Balanchine commented, 'Yes – he's short.
He's a very short brother!'

They were fond of each other and Andrey described to George
the manner of their father's death. Meliton was seventy-six in
1937 and gangrene was diagnosed in his leg. The doctors
prepared for amputation but were met by a point-blank refusal.
Losing patience, his own doctor said, 'If you don't have the
operation you'll be dead in two days', to which Meliton replied,
'So be it . . . death is a beautiful girl who is going to come and
take me in her arms. I look forward to the experience.' He died
two days later. Balanchine was touched and charmed by this
story – it was the old, authentic Meliton, just as he remembered
him.

The fondness between the brothers did not encompass
Andrey's musical talents. George listened to several of his
compositions and was quite unable to enthuse or, indeed, to say
anything, and his brother was deeply hurt. Earlier in the tour
George had considered the inclusion of a piano concerto by
Andrey in one of his Georgian programmes, but now this idea
came to nothing, to Bob Irving's relief. Andrey suffered another
unhappy moment when his daughter danced for George. She

and her family had hopes of a career in the West, perhaps under
the banner of the American school and company, but her uncle
dashed any further thoughts of this kind – he found her talent
barely average and her training poor. Admittedly it was a
difficult situation for him, but Balanchine seems to have had no
gift of compassion in the manner of his assessment. It is sad that
his only remaining family were shown the harsh side of his
nature.

During the Russian tour this harshness became apparent on
public occasions. In a quiet, controlled way Balanchine showed
signs of becoming an autocrat and his treatment of questions
from the press and from Russian colleagues was often high-
handed. On his arrival at Moscow airport, where he and the
company received a rapturous reception, an interviewer from
Radio Moscow said, 'Welcome to Moscow, home of the classic
ballet', to which Balanchine replied, 'I beg your pardon –
Russia is the home of romantic ballet. The home of classic ballet
is now America.' To borrow Balanchine's favourite use of
gastronomic analogy, this is like arriving, by invitation, at a
celebrated Italian restaurant and telling the chef that the home
of perfect pasta is in your own house. It was unnecessary and
deeply discourteous. There is no doubt that Balanchine was
under great strain while in Russia but, as with many people
who gain power, he was now allowing it to dictate his own
behaviour.

19
Obsession

The New York City Ballet had become a strong and vital entity. The imbalance of its early years, when the dancing of the women had been all-important, was a thing of the past and the company now had three splendid leading male dancers in Edward Villella, Arthur Mitchell and Jacques d'Amboise. The triumphant Russian tour was followed by yet more success at home and the future looked bright. The year 1963 brought two important people to Balanchine in his work, one old friend and one new.

The long and exceptionally enjoyable dancing career of Alexandra Danilova was now over and she came to teach at the school and to collaborate in revivals of old classic ballets. She had lived in New York for some years and had always kept in touch with George, so this was a warm and happy partnership for them both. His new friend was a young woman called Barbara Horgan, who became his secretary and personal assistant; she remained with him for the rest of his life and is still with the company today.

She wandered into the ballet world unexpectedly. While a drama student at Columbia University, she met several City dancers at various parties and one day found herself caught up in a group going to City Center. There she was introduced to Betty Cage, the general manager of the company, who was looking for a secretary and offered her the job. She had never thought about becoming a secretary, but the atmosphere at City

Center attracted her and she accepted. She was not disappointed in her decision, and Betty Cage wasn't either. Ten
years later Balanchine came into her office, talked for a little,
asked her if she would like to work for him – and that was that.
The prospect of working with him didn't intimidate her in the
least – she says with amusement, that at the time she 'had no
idea that he was a genius'.

Today she is a fair-haired woman of charm and authority,
looking twenty years younger than she should. She loved
working for Balanchine and was to be his most important single
support in his later, failing years. But she speaks with thankful-
ness of 'never having been a dancer' and 'never having that
relationship with him'. With amused detachment she watched
young female dancers jockeying for position and vying with
each other to attract his particular attention; she describes
entering one of his classes as 'going through a wall of scent!' He
may not have been altogether dissatisfied with this state of
affairs – though devoted to him, Barbara Horgan thought him a
man of considerable vanity.

One young girl had no need to catch his eye, because she
attracted Balanchine's attention immediately. Her quiet, grave
face, her physique and her superb classical talent appealed
strongly to him, and in 1963 he adapted for her a ballet
originally intended for Diana Adams – Stravinsky's *Movements
for Piano and Orchestra*. When she danced this with Jacques
d'Amboise they made a great impression – Suzanne Farrell was
seen by the public, the press and the choreographer himself as
the archetypal Balanchine dancer. She was the perfect instrument for the new ballets he wanted to create, and as the 1960s
progressed he wrote one after another almost exclusively for
her. They shared a marvellous working relationship and her
devotion to his teaching and his ballets was absolute. This
naturally delighted him, as did her restrained personality and
her sense of humour.

The Stravinsky was followed later that year by Tchaikovsky's
Meditation. In the spring of 1964 the company opened the new
and luxurious State Theater at Lincoln Center – the stage had
been built with Balanchine's specifications in mind – and
Suzanne Farrell danced in the first presentation in the new

house, *Clarinade*, with music by Morton Gould for Benny
Goodman, and with Benny himself as soloist. Her next ballet
was a revival of *Ballet Imperial*. In 1965 came the full-length
Don Quixote and her Dulcinea; the mime role of the Don,
originally played by Richard Rapp, was taken over by Balanchine himself on several occasions. In Bob Irving's words, 'it
was heavy-going and patchy', with 'a long and ungrateful score
by Nicolas Nabokov'. In 1966, three Stravinsky ballets were
written for Suzanne Farrell – *Variations*, *Elégie* and *Ragtime II*.
In 1967 came the Diamonds section of his full-length *Jewels*,
followed in 1968 by three ballets – *Metastaseis and Pitho-
prakta*, a new, extended version of *Slaughter on Tenth Avenue*
(from *On Your Toes*) and another Stravinsky, *Requiem Canti-
cles* – in memory of Martin Luther King.

Balanchine was obsessed. During these years, only two
ballets and several pas de deux were created for other dancers,
and it was clear to everyone that Balanchine's commitment was
to one dancer alone. Melissa Hayden felt pushed on one side;
Maria felt the same, yet says generously, 'But, when all the
ballets were made for me, everyone else must have felt like
this.' It reached the point when no jumps would be given in
classes because 'Suzanne has a bad knee'. Favouritism in ballet
companies is a strange phenomenon, yet all too common.
Diaghilev directed his Ballets Russes in this way, and Ninette
de Valois directed her company in this way. Now, here was
Balanchine in the same trap, but falling into it more deeply than
before.

In 1969, at the age of sixty-five, he seemed to take leave of his
senses. Having made generous settlements on Tanaquil
LeClercq, he rushed to Mexico for a divorce, then back to New
York to ask Suzanne Farrell to marry him. She was twenty-four.
Brigitta speaks of a moment during her marriage to Balanchine
when George, reading a newspaper story, said, 'How ridiculous
it is when an old man marries a young girl.' Like many old men,
he had forgotten. Suzanne Farrell's behaviour was impeccable.
She had fallen in love with a handsome young member of the
company, Paul Mejia, and intended to marry him. She refused
Balanchine. For him the resulting days and weeks were like the
torments of Diaghilev after the defection of Massine.

Contracted to the Hamburg State Opera to direct and stage dances for Glinka's *Ruslan and Ludmilla* in February 1969, he left America in a mood of anger and despair, half hoping never to return. Many people were worried about him at this time – none more so than Barbara Horgan, who had watched his obsession from the beginning. Many, also, felt strongly for Tanaquil LeClercq – Maria speaks of how bitterly she felt her abandonment, and no wonder. When the day of the Mejia wedding came, Barbara Horgan felt she must attend it, must see it happen; then – as she put it – she would have 'exorcized' all the past years. She returned home from the reception to find her telephone ringing – it was Balanchine in Hamburg, shouting, 'You've betrayed me.' She explained to him exactly why she had gone to the wedding, and then, more calmly, he asked her to fly to Hamburg the next day. When she rang the airline office she discovered that he had already booked her ticket. He met her plane and they ate breakfast together, Balanchine in an implacable state and vowing never to return to America.

Gradually, over the next two weeks, she brought him to a near-acceptance of the situation. She was the right person, in the right place, at the right time – and she enjoyed her visit and his company, which was an unexpected treat. They returned to New York in April and Balanchine was soon hard at work. Suzanne and Paul Mejia left the company to dance first in Canada, and then with the Maurice Béjart Ballet in Belgium. Balanchine had made it clear that Mejia need not expect leading roles at the State Theater – a little mean, perhaps, but one can understand this response from an ageing and rejected suitor. There was a comic postscript to the whole business: soon after Balanchine's return from Germany he met his old flame Shura Danilova in the street – yet again. After chatting for a few minutes he turned to go, saying, 'Well, I won't be marrying again, thank you ve-e-ery much!' And this time he meant it.

He was, however, to have one more close friendship. In 1962, when he was in Hamburg for *Eugen Onegin*, a big, twenty-one-year-old German girl, carrying a letter of introduction from Lotte Lenya, arrived for an audition. Karin von Aroldingen was athletic, powerful and unlikely. Balanchine told her flatly that he did not care for her dancing and that there was no chance of a place in his company. Back in New York he changed his mind, and she joined the ballet later in the year. She was a tremendously hard worker but had difficulty with the English language. When she met and decided to marry a real estate broker called Morton Gerwitz in 1965, she told Barbara Horgan it was because she 'couldn't bear to go on talking on the telephone'. When she became pregnant, Karin von Aroldingen seemed to disregard the whole process; she danced in performances until her sixth month, took classes until her eighth, and four weeks after the birth of her daughter rejoined the company. But she was quite changed – the big German frame was trimmed down, she was svelte and sleek and glamorous. And she worked harder than ever.

Balanchine was attracted to her and gained her complete devotion. Barbara Horgan speaks of this devotion and also of his adamant decision never to marry again. It amused him to give a whimsical reason: 'I like to get up very early in the morning, to wander about with no clothes on and to sit, naked, playing solitaire – no woman will put up with that.' He had his own New York apartment and he bought a condominium in Southampton, Long Island, beside one owned by the Gerwitz family, whom he visited regularly. In this way the loneliness of Balanchine's old age was made easier – the loneliness of someone who has never given full value to relationships or tried hard enough to preserve them.

In 1969, one other dancer of importance joined the City Ballet. Peter Martins, from Denmark, was – and is – fair-haired and exceptionally good-looking and his talents equal his appearance. He came to the company as a principal dancer, which suggests that Balanchine found his work more than acceptable. But for his first two years he was given a very rough ride indeed, and made to feel so foolish and useless that he seriously considered resigning from the company. He has written about this experience, frankly and generously, shouldering the blame himself. He speaks of his failure to submit himself completely to Balanchine's teaching, of his wish to make his work look 'beautiful' when Balanchine often wanted the reverse, and of his wretched feelings of humiliation when he was mocked and mercilessly imitated in front of the whole company. No situation of this kind is ever one-sided, and I think he protests his guilt too much. Perhaps he is right when he states that he was not submissive enough in the beginning, but nothing can justify the type of public humiliation he describes. Behaviour of this kind is not unknown in ballet companies and it shows that Balanchine, like many others, was using his power in a sarcastic and cruel way.

An actor in the dramatic theatre, every emotion bared and on display, is probably the most vulnerable performer of all. But there is also vulnerability in the way a dancer dances, physique and personal idiosyncrasy of movement being individual to each one. It is unforgivable when a director, teacher or choreographer, using his or her superior status, makes a deliberate attempt to break and destroy. It is also foolish, as such behaviour says so much more about the perpetrator than about the victim. I see this in the accounts of Balanchine's treatment of Peter Martins, and at the same time am aware of the irony of my opinion, having myself been treated by him so differently.

Luckily, Peter Martins weathered these years, becoming the *danseur noble* of the City Ballet and, after Balanchine's death, co-director with Jerome Robbins. Barbara Horgan, who was aware of his early difficulties, feels that Balanchine's behaviour stemmed from the impatience of age – 'He never wanted to give time to people or to bother about their feelings.' Shura Danilova says simply, 'He was a Georgian – and a very cruel man.' Perhaps, in fairness, one should also remember his tenderness and devotion to Tanaquil LeClercq in the first years after her illness when, the doctors having given up in despair, he was the one who kept her going, forcing her to move around, to do things, and teaching her how to accomplish the task of moving from bed to wheelchair and back without help from anyone. So much in human behaviour is contradictory, and Balanchine was no exception to the rule.

20

Festivals

In the decade of the 1970s Balanchine appeared to have everything. The quality and prestige of his school and company were universally recognized, his own preservation and enhancement of the classic ballet were appreciated as unique, and honours were showered on him. He had the satisfaction of knowing that it was not only New York that demonstrated his teaching and dance philosophy: his many visits to major American cities across the continent, when he had not only given classes but held seminars for teachers and students, ensured that his methods were now the yardstick for them all. His ballets were danced in many countries, frequently staged by himself; his company's foreign tours, including a second visit to Russia, were enthusiastically received, and at home he now had a perfect showcase for his work – the State Theater. He lacked only two things, youth and health. As he approached his seventies he could hardly expect the former, but his increasingly poor health became a great burden.

He had, in fact, been singularly lucky after his early tuberculosis and collapsed lung. His energy, quite unimpaired, had continued through the first years of the 1970s. In 1972 it reached its peak with the presentation of ten ballets for the posthumous ninetieth birthday celebrations for Igor Stravinsky. Nine of these were new works, choreographed and rehearsed within a few weeks: Sonata; Symphony in Three Movements; Violin Concerto; a new Divertimento to music from Baiser de la

Fée; *Scherzo à la Russe*; *Duo Concertant*; *Pulcinella*; *Choral Variations on Bach's Von Himmel Hoch*; and *Symphony of Psalms*, a presentation with dancers assembled on stage with singers. Balanchine also revived his *Danses Concertantes*, giving it his well-known treatment of a choreographic facelift. He kept an eye on twelve productions contributed by other choreographers, who included Jerome Robbins and Todd Bolender, and there were performances of famous earlier ballets – *Apollo*, *Orpheus*, *Firebird*, *Agon*, *Capriccio for Piano and Orchestra*, *Monumentum Pro Gesualdo* and *Movements for Piano and Orchestra*. Bob Irving speaks of the week of the Festival performances as 'the highest point in my time with the New York City company', and Richard Buckle, in the London *Sunday Times*, waxed lyrical. It was a high point for everyone; for Balanchine, at sixty-eight, a great achievement and a wonderful stimulation for his dancers. The composer 'should have died hereafter' – he would have loved his week.

Ballet Imperial was revived yet again in 1973, but now it was entitled *Tchaikovsky Piano Concerto No. 2*, and décor and costumes were discarded. The dancers wore practice clothes – chiffon tunics for the women – and they performed in front of a plain backcloth. I felt twinges of envy when I read of this alteration. At Covent Garden, in 1950, I had found the stiff, formal tutus uncomfortable and cumbersome for the exact execution of the tricky choreography, and I also thought that they masked many of the movements. To have given performances of this marvellous ballet in practice costume would have been a rare pleasure. Balanchine's awareness of his lack of taste in décor and dress may well have led to the paring down of many of his later productions. More and more he used practice clothes and simple chiffon shifts, together with austere backcloths, and he sometimes discarded titles for new ballets, preferring the music's own name and form.

There is no doubt that his abstract ballets looked their best when dressed so simply. With such choreography one wants no distraction of any kind, and it is the perfect dress from the dancer's point of view. But one criticism could be heard from both press and public. All Balanchine's female dancers wore their hair scraped back from the face and knotted tightly at the back of the head. It was such a severe effect that they were sometimes described as 'the pinhead brigade'. A mass of hair is a problem for a dancer, because it must be neat and secure for all the spinning and pirouetting involved. But this was surely going too far. I found it astonishingly ugly, giving the wrong proportion to the head vis à vis the body. Then, occasionally, Balanchine would go to the other extreme and dancers would leap across the stage with loose hair flying into their eyes, their mouths and their partners' faces. Only in a few of his ballets have I seen this small but important detail treated in both a practical and attractive way.

Balanchine visited Berlin in February 1973 to stage a production of Borodin's *Prince Igor* and, back in New York, created a last ballet, *Cortège Hongrois*, for Melissa Hayden before her retirement in May. Also in May, he collaborated with Edward Villella on *Begin the Beguine* at the Philharmonic Hall for an evening of Cole Porter celebration, *Salute to Cole*. His sixty-nine years may have brought about changes in his behaviour, but they were not causing him to fossilize professionally.

On his seventieth birthday he was engaged in the arrangement of a very odd piece – a short ballet with a long name, *Variations pour une Porte et un Soupir*; the music described on the programme as 'Sonority by Pierre Henry', had been originally composed and performed in 1963. There were two dancers, Karin von Aroldingen as the Door and John Clifford as the Sigh, but the leading rôle seems to have been performed by the Door's gigantic black skirt, which covered the stage, heaving and palpitating throughout the performance. It sounded to me, as its reception seems to have reflected, a faintly repellent piece and I asked Lincoln Kirstein for his view. Looking disdainful and manic, he said, 'Oh, that was rubbish – just rubbish. We often did things like that.'

As an antidote to this production, Balanchine and Danilova staged the Delibes, full-length *Coppélia* in July 1974. In many ways an old warhorse, it has always been a great public favourite, and the company was fortunate to have a charming and expert Swanhilda and Franz, Patricia McBride and Helgi Tomasson, and the Dr Coppélius of Shaun O'Brien. Balanchine and Danilova had returned to the original conception of this ballet as a fantasy for children and, as Clive Barnes wrote in *The New York Times*, 'He understands the child's need for horror. Coppélius is made into a serious Hoffmannesque character, full of Gothic, creepy horror.'

The English Ballet, during the war and post-war years, had kept this old classic alive with a production containing a pantomime dame Coppélius. It was an interpretation of sheer buffoonery – very funny at a first viewing, a crashing bore thereafter. It completely destroyed the mood and balance of the ballet and was a peculiar lapse of taste and judgement in a company devoted to tradition. In New York, Balanchine and Danilova restored the sinister, unknown element in their re-creation of Dr Coppélius. Theirs was a fruitful partnership: Shura could remember and demonstrate many small details of early productions, while George worked on the wider canvas. Their *Coppélia* was a much admired addition to the repertoire.

Before the end of the year, Balanchine – remaining in his traditional vein – arranged dances for *Boris Godunov* at the Metropolitan Opera House. This was not the old house where he had suffered so miserably in the 1930s, but now the spanking new one at Lincoln Center. In May 1975 there was another Festival – a week dedicated to the music of Maurice Ravel. This raised some surprised eyebrows. Why Ravel? 'Why not Ravel?' snapped Balanchine to a reporter. Was he really enamoured of Ravel's music, or was his early apathy still rankling? I think the latter. Balanchine was by far the most musical of choreographers, but he had begun to believe his own myth as the only musical choreographer in the world. No one else may have been aware of his youthful lapse, but he had to put it right for himself.

In the event, the Festival was only a semi-success. *L'Enfant et les Sortilèges* appeared again in a third staging, and was followed by *Sonatine, Shéhérazade, Le Tombeau de Couperin, Tzigane, Gaspard de la Nuit* and *Rhapsodie Espagnole*. I did not see these productions myself but can understand why one critic wrote, 'The magic was missing.' By now Balanchine was seventy-one. Age, certainly, must have had its effect, but I think that Ravel's shimmering music, which has the same quality as the paintings of the Impressionists, was more difficult for

Balanchine than the music of Mozart, Tchaikovsky and Stravinsky. An exception, however, was his earlier and successful
La Valse in which Tanaquil LeClercq had excelled. But Ravel
composed *La Valse* for Diaghilev and for a ballet, and though it
was not used – Diaghilev considered it unsuitable – it is
undoubtedly music for dancing. To attempt a staging of an
intangible, atmospheric work like *Gaspard de la Nuit* is very
different; it may have defeated both choreographer and public
alike. *Tzigane* was written for a returning prodigal – Suzanne
Farrell. She had rejoined the company after a reconciliation
with Balanchine at Saratoga Springs, where the company
danced each summer. But she came back alone, for Balanchine
refused to re-engage Paul Mejia, who later joined Maria Tallchief in Chicago as co-director of her Chicago Ballet.

Madame Giscard d'Estaing, wife of the French President, was
in the audience for the opening gala of the Ravel Festival – it
was a week of honour to the French. After the performance
Balanchine was decorated with the Légion d'Honneur and soon
he received another prize, the Distinguished Service Award,
from the American National Institute of Arts and Letters.
However pleased he may have been by this recognition, he
adopted a strange way of showing it. Mrs Molostwoff tells of a
dinner given in his honour at one of New York's grand hotels.
The artistic élite of the city was seated waiting for the arrival of
its distinguished guest when he came into the lobby, dressed
soberly but with an open-necked shirt and cravat in place of a
tie. The doorman refused to let him in. Balanchine explained
who he was and why he was there, but with apologies the
doorman told him that a tie was essential. He then produced
several from a drawer, inviting Balanchine to choose, whereupon the guest of honour turned and walked out of the hotel. He
went to a hamburger restaurant nearby, ate his dinner alone and
returned to his apartment. The next day everyone was talking
about his solitary dinner.

It was all very petty and silly, quite apart from the display of
rudeness to his hosts, but my greatest surprise was in the telling
by Mrs Molostwoff. She thought it a wonderful story and
entirely to Balanchine's credit. Barbara Horgan speaks of a
similar episode which involved herself. Balanchine had

promised to take her to dine at New York's Maxim's restaurant – she had never been there and was thrilled. When she arrived, he was waiting for her, again without a tie. Again he refused the management's offer to lend him one and, without a thought for her, took her round the corner to a small bar-restaurant. Restaurants seem to have brought out the worst in him. Sometimes, in Italian trattorias offering every variety of spaghetti, she would hear him demanding absolutely plain spaghetti with a little butter, making a fuss and causing despondency among the staff. As she says, 'It was so silly – he could easily have made it for himself at home.'

Balanchine had become arrogant, and his arrogance always reached a peak with the press. He was contemptuous of the often silly questions invariably put to him and one can sympathize with this, though not with the sarcasm and perversity of many of his replies. His command of English was never perfect, and perhaps he was more cutting than he meant to be; and the disease which finally killed him may have affected his judgement much earlier than anyone realized. Even so, he diminished himself by an all-powerful, all-knowing attitude. This had been particularly noticeable when he had visited Russia for the second tour in 1972. Barbara Horgan remembers occasions when, seated at a table for press conferences or with dancers and teachers from Russian companies, Balanchine would play the game of veiled half-truths and social niceties, then slam his hand down on the table and rap out a final dictatorial statement. It must have been an unnerving experience for his hosts.

Still, in spite of age, the ballets flowed on – not with the same effervescence, and increasingly in collaboration with one or another choreographer, but every now and then with a rare quality. For the Bicentennial he staged a topical ballet, *Union Jack*, much appreciated in America but frowned upon in England. I found the first part of this work quite magical. Slow drumbeats, slow marching, the Scottish regiments coming to the stage one after another, slowly, inexorably, the marvellous Scottish dress in silhouette – then seen, as the lights were raised, in their sombre-brilliant colours. Then the Scots melodies and the haunting laments: all Scots feel an incurable romanticism about their land, their history and culture, and

Balanchine had created a realization of this which brought me close to tears.

In 1977 he had a sensational success with *Vienna Waltzes*, using music by Johann Strauss the younger, Franz Léhar and Richard Strauss. The last, *Rosenkavalier*, section of the ballet is the real pearl: a chandeliered ballroom enclosed by giant mirrored walls, reflecting the swirl of a sea of waltzing couples and with Suzanne Farrell, at her most grave and beautiful, at the centre. Here one can find no fault with Balanchine's visual taste – the whole effect was ravishing and it captivated everyone who saw it.

But he was not content to rest on safe, popular ballets. In January 1978, after arranging a ballet for a dancer of exceptional brio, Merrill Ashley, he choreographed one of his most difficult and spartan works – *Kammermusik No. 2*, to a score by Paul Hindemith. There were no concessions to beauty or warmth. In shifts and practice dress, without scenery, the dancers performed his most extreme and complex inventions, and even Lincoln Kirstein described the effect as 'slightly repellent, inhuman, desperate, insistent, harshly deliberate – even cruel'.

Balanchine was not well when he worked on this production. Now seventy-four, he was plagued by bouts of dizziness and exhaustion, and in March he had a heart attack – not a serious one, but enough to force him into hospital for two weeks. Doctors talked to him of the benefits of rest, a slower pace of life, possible retirement, and during April he seems to have listened to their advice. He stayed quietly in his apartment and behaved like a model patient, but as soon as his strength and well-being returned he was off to the theatre to work as hard as ever. But it was false strength. His energy was not as it had been, his concentration was affected and he tired quickly, all of which deeply depressed him. His appearance altered too. His hair had been whitening for some time, but now the famous aquiline profile became puffy and, for the only time in his life his body looked heavy, even fat. He was more ill than he, or anyone near him, realized.

21
Last Days

A dazzling newcomer made his first appearance with the City Ballet in July 1978 – Mikhail Baryshnikov. This exceptional thirty-year-old dancer had defected from the Soviet Union in 1974; he had then danced in western Europe before settling in America, where he joined Ballet Theater to rapturous acclaim. There had been much speculation about his possible move from Ballet Theater to Balanchine, not least between the two protagonists themselves, and now it was accomplished. Most writings about Balanchine stress his dislike of stars, and in one sense this is true. He disliked the 'starry' star – the man or woman who brings the panoply of stardom on to the stage, dancing only set, bravura pieces or appearing, ever more idiosyncratically, in an old classic, with the rest of the cast in half-light behind them. But he loved star quality, as we all do, and his company never lacked it with dancers like Maria Tallchief, Tanaquil LeClercq, Peter Martins and Merrill Ashley. Balanchine always used star quality in the service of his ballets rather than in isolated bravura posturings, and perhaps this confused the public more than he knew.

There is no doubting Baryshnikov's stardom. He cannot help being a solo performer, any more than others less fortunate can help fading into the background. He had been given star treatment with Ballet Theater and would be inhuman if he hadn't enjoyed it. But he wanted to work with Balanchine and so became another member of his company at the normal salary for a principal. The two Russians took to each other at once, always spoke in their own language, and saw much of each other socially as well as professionally. Baryshnikov was fascinated by the sparseness of Balanchine's life – the minimal possessions and memorabilia, coupled with his love of superb food and wine. But he was unprepared for the frailty and recurring illness which blighted their working relationship. His hopes of being part of Balanchine's unique creative work were now an impossibility.

By the autumn of 1978 Balanchine had developed angina and his increasing exhaustion and painful attacks were causing alarm. He dragged himself through as much teaching and rehearsal as possible, but it was obvious that treatment was necessary. He had a new doctor, the young Edith Langner, who understood his way of life as she had treated Barbara Horgan and several members of the company. Balanchine liked her and felt comfortable with her, but she fared no better than her predecessors when she attempted to cut down on the rich, delicious menus on which he had thrived for so long. Nevertheless he was frightened by his condition, and frightened still more by talk of a possible angiogram which might show the necessity for heart bypass surgery.

He tried to put all thoughts of health from his mind and to keep his concentration centred on two productions for the New York City Opera at the State Theater. Purcell's *Dido and Aeneas* was to be presented in April 1979, with dances by Peter Martins under Balanchine's co-direction with Frank Corsaro. A ballet was required to complete a double bill, and Balanchine decided on the suite *Le Bourgeois Gentilhomme* by Richard Strauss. It was a score he knew well, having made two earlier productions, but now he was unable to tackle it alone and he asked Jerome Robbins for his collaboration. Students from the school danced as the corps de ballet, and Patricia McBride and Jean-Pierre Bonnefous, together with Rudolf Nureyev, danced the three principal roles.

Nureyev had danced in several Balanchine ballets with other companies and had enjoyed the experience, but he had never worked personally with George. This also proved to be a pleasure, though inevitably, because of Balanchine's health, his

contribution was much less than Nureyev would have liked.
Unluckily, the ballet failed with both public and critics: an
excellent writer, Arlene Croce, described the production as 'a
pretentious embarrassment' and was unable to see 'any evidence of a successful collaboration between the star and the
choreographers'. Whether Balanchine read reviews like this we
don't know (he always liked to say that he didn't) but an
amended version of the ballet was presented the following year,
with Peter Martins replacing Nureyev. Its reception seems to
have been much warmer.

The company's spring season opened in May with a bomb-
shell new version of Balanchine's hallowed *Apollo*, Baryshnikov dancing the title role. No one could believe it. It was
truncated and cut about in an apparently savage way and the
public – liking what it knows and what it expects to see – was
amazed and shocked. To the protesting critics Balanchine
retorted, 'I don't have to explain why I change things. I can do
with my ballets whatever I like.' But then, foolishly, he went on
to explain and justify, sometimes snappily and on the defen-
sive, but once, I think, making a very telling point. In answer to
nostalgic wailings, he said that if today's public could see the
original of 1928, 'they would laugh their heads off at how it
used to be'. This is true. Taste and the beholder's eye change
dramatically over the years, and in terms of performance it
could be a mixed blessing that we cannot now see Pavlova,
Nijinsky, Henry Irving and Ellen Terry. Their legendary reputa-
tions are safe, and can only grow with time.

By the end of May Balanchine was in severe pain, and even
the smallest exertion was beyond him. He could ignore it no
longer; he entered hospital for the dreaded angiogram, and
within a week he was given triple bypass surgery. His fear of the
operation was still as great, but he was comforted by the
knowledge of Lincoln Kirstein's similar bypass a few years
earlier which had been a complete success. In July he was
allowed to go to his apartment in Southampton to recuperate
and he stayed there quietly, not attempting to travel to Saratoga
Springs for the company's annual summer season. But, for a
London season scheduled for September, he had different
plans. Despite cataracts in both eyes and a strangely worrying

inability to keep his balance, he accompanied his dancers to Covent Garden, and many English friends found him in good heart and with a certain vigour and strength.

The public gave the company a great reception, while the critics niggled away as usual. A peculiar chauvinism characterized the London circle of dancers, balletomanes and critics whenever the Americans presented a season. The self-satisfied attitude of the English ballet seemed to spill over into many reviews, and Balanchine's productions were always inflammatory. But sniping at American technique was foolish, for this was the one aspect of the company which deserved only praise, their technique being infinitely superior to everyone else's. There was a last ludicrous exchange between Balanchine and the critic Alexander Bland, quoted by Bernard Taper. Speaking of his fondness for London and how he had once thought of settling there, George said that it was probably a good thing that he hadn't done so – he really lacked sufficient dignity for a country where 'if you are awake it is already vulgar'. This sally met with a tight-lipped reception and later, in a lather of smugness, Bland wrote, 'Though technically fastidious, he certainly lacks the regulator of good taste, which is one of Britain's hallmarks.'

At home in New York throughout 1980, Balanchine's improved health permitted him to work with the company on two revivals and to choreograph two new ballets without collaboration of any kind. *Robert Schumann's Davidsbündler-tänze* was the last complete ballet he wrote, at the age of seventy-six, and only the second time that he had used the music of Schumann. This work, written for four couples who seem to represent Robert and his wife, Clara, in various moods and episodes from their lives, marked a change in Balanchine. The flow of movement was still evident, with every now and then a pose, a turning of one dancer to another, a quiet, drifting walk away from the stage – all inimitable. But there was a feeling of sadness, of resignation, from the first note to the last. For the first time he seemed to reveal an awareness of his own mortality.

His choice of Schumann was interesting, as was his choice the following year of Tchaikovsky, in a festival dedicated to the

Russian composer. Schumann was an attempted suicide who
died tragically in an asylum for the insane, and Tchaikovsky,
after a major homosexual indiscretion, was forced to commit
suicide by a tribunal of his peers. Balanchine – the quiet,
equable George, with his low voice and sharp, prankish
humour – was now, in old age, drawn to these two tragic men.
He had always been so self-assured, so self-centred and so
confident in his view of life. His own sad condition made this
impossible to sustain, and now for the first time he appreciated
the sadness of other lives.

Those who were near Balanchine in these last years were
deeply affected by the experience. Maria Tallchief speaks of the
change in the work of the company and of her own distress at
realizing that Balanchine could no longer see that his work was
being performed incorrectly. Bob Irving speaks of the pathos of
watching his slow but inexorable deterioration. Though his eye
cataracts were removed over a period of months, his sight was
only partially improved, and his loss of balance rapidly increased. This was the hardest blow of all for a man who taught
and rehearsed his dancers through personal demonstration;
now he could barely rise from his chair. He often wore a jacket
with a red elbow patch. When he visited Dr Langner in her
consulting room, regardless of anything he might or might not
say to her, she would always know his exact condition from the
red elbow marks dotted along her long, white-painted corridor.

Another blow struck this ill old man in the winter of 1980.
Four years earlier his orchestral musicians had gone on strike
for six weeks, causing disruption and financial difficulty. Now
his own dancers voted to strike for more money; Balanchine
could hardly believe it. In her exceptional book *Winter Season*,
Toni Bentley, one of his dancers, describes what happened. The
company was split on the issue: at the vote meeting less than
half the company was present, of whom twenty-six voted for a
strike and eighteen against. After an initial burst of anger,
Balanchine confronted the full company at the end of a daily
class. He spoke in a quiet, friendly manner, reminding them of
the development of the company to its present status, of the
offer from Kirstein and himself, which was final, and also of the
small strike majority. What he wanted was a full vote, a clear

majority one way or the other, and he ended with: 'Yes or no –
from a hundred and five.'

Toni Bentley writes of the sinking hearts of the dancers
gathered round him, thinking that he might call for a show of
hands then and there; but he didn't. A box was provided for
their written votes, and a week later the company had accepted
a slightly improved offer from the management. Balanchine
must have been aware that there were now many faces in his
company that he couldn't recognize – dancers who had rarely
seen him and who did not know him. The old close-knit, family
atmosphere was quite gone – he was like a stranger in his own
house.

The Tchaikovsky Festival in 1981 was as sombre as the 1972
Stravinsky Festival had been joyous. The culmination was an
arrangement by Balanchine of the *Adagio Lamentoso* from the
Symphony No. 6, the Pathétique. The dancers portrayed black-
clad monks and white angels with miraculously tall wings, and
later the English critic Clement Crisp wrote that 'Balanchine the
creator said his farewell to us at the end of the 1981 Tchaikovsky Festival.' But his life dragged on, and by the early spring
of 1982 his condition was much worse. His failing sight made
reading and watching television almost impossible; his hearing
was affected with an often intolerable jangling and grinding
noise in his head, and his sense of balance was destroyed. He
was given complete neurological examinations but none of the
extensive tests gave any clue to his malady. The doctors
remained in the dark and could do nothing to help him.

There was to be one last festival, one he had planned several
years earlier, to celebrate the centenary of Igor Stravinsky. Four
of his own ballets were presented, among many others, and
Brigitta came to perform the spoken rôle in the lyric drama
Perséphone. She remembers George being present at the rehearsals but quite unable to take part, and how the staging had to be
made by John Taras and herself. Karin von Aroldingen was cast
as the Spirit of Perséphone, and when movement and dances
were rehearsed with her Brigitta saw the German dancer 'draw'
choreography from Balanchine in some strange way. She found
this slightly sinister. When he appeared, holding firmly to the
curtain, for the last-night calls and the great reception for

himself, it was the last time the public would ever see him.

He still lived alone in his New York apartment, and for some time Barbara Horgan had been worried about his safety. She was troubled by the loose rugs he liked in preference to fitted carpets, by a large glass table in his drawing room, and by the entrance to his front door where there were five unprotected steps. In the autumn of 1982 he had two falls and she decided that railings for the steps were essential. Work was started and the rails installed in November, as Balanchine, inside the apartment and moving to answer the telephone, fell again – this time more seriously. He fractured four ribs and his left wrist and was taken to the Roosevelt Hospital. He never used the railings.

He lay in his hospital bed for five months. At first he talked frequently about coming home and resuming work, then less, and then, if he mentioned this at all, it was always 'next week' or 'next month'. He was very ill much of the time, his memory and power of speech often deserting him completely, but his room was always filled with visitors. Barbara Horgan speaks of the generosity of the hospital authorities, who waived almost every rule and regulation at this time; she was continually involved with the staff as she had to arrange for day and night nurses during this long period. Dancers and wives all came to see him – Brigitta, Tamara, Maria, Shura Danilova and, of course, the company. Karin von Aroldingen was perhaps his greatest comfort: she attended him devotedly and even at his lowest moments he always recognized her step in the corridor before she entered his room. Barbara Horgan speaks particularly of Maria and Shura. Maria was more outwardly upset than anyone, 'near hysteria' each time she left his room and always in tears when she telephoned from Chicago. But Danilova was the most affecting of all. She came only once to the hospital, and when she left his room she said, 'I won't come here again – I have said goodbye to him.' Watching her walk slowly away, Barbara Horgan felt a great sorrow for Shura, realizing that she was losing her oldest and dearest friend.

Epilogue

George Balanchine died on 30 April 1983. In his last weeks he had become slim and unlined, like a young man. He was buried in a small cemetery of his own choice in Sag Harbour, Long Island, after a funeral service in the Cathedral of Our Lady of the Sign, which overflowed with more than a thousand mourners. Six months later, on All Souls' Day, a memorial service was held in the Anglican Cathedral of St John the Divine on Amsterdam Avenue, not far from Lincoln Center and the State Theater. The American ballet world, many other artists and members of the public came to pay a last tribute to him. His favourite Mozart Requiem was played, and the service ended with anthems sung by the Russian Orthodox Choir, music which had meant so much to him in his St Petersburg childhood.

But this did not signal the ending of his work. Today, his influence is as strong as ever, and everything that he gave to the ballet in his prolific life has changed our perception of the art. His great gifts as a teacher can now be seen as paramount: across America and in Europe many of his original New York dancers are teaching his inimitable style and technique in schools, colleges and companies. He may not have wished his ballets to last, believing them to be essentially ephemeral, but his style cannot die and that would have pleased him.

For those nearest to him at the time of his death, the medical consequences were distressing. The doctors had been baffled by his long illness; they realized that there was cerebellar degenerative disease but they had no idea of its cause, so an autopsy was performed and his brain removed. It was placed in a jar of formalin for ten days, then sliced in layers and tissue removed and treated for study under a microscope. In a tiny section of brain they found a pink circle called *kuru plaque*, the sign of a rare family of virus diseases. This was the clue – though pneumonia had hastened the end, Balanchine had died from Creutzfeldt-Jakob's disease, a slow and so far untreatable condition. It is extremely difficult to detect in a living patient, and to complicate it further Balanchine's symptoms appeared in reverse order to the accepted pattern. This information was only made public because of wild speculation about the nature of his illness which circled New York. Finally, Barbara Horgan, Balanchine's executrix, put an end to all rumours by granting a public hearing and lecture in Columbia University's College of Physicians and Surgeons. It took place on the first anniversary of his death and was published a week later in the *Science Times*, part of *The New York Times*.

Within the City Ballet the transition period was difficult. Balanchine had refused to name a successor, and for several years there had been confusion among members and ex-members of the company who considered their own qualifications to be strong. Latterly, the Danish Peter Martins had seemed the natural choice, and Balanchine – though never committing himself – had given the impression of agreeing with such a choice. There was, however, Jerome Robbins, senior in every way, and the board had a problem. This was resolved by the appointment of both men as co-balletmasters-in-chief; Peter Martins in charge of artistic policy and administration, and Jerome Robbins as artistic adviser and principal choreographer. There was only one loss in this arrangement – Peter Martins could no longer continue his dancing career, choosing to sacrifice it to the continuation of Balanchine's work.

Today there is inevitable criticism. Lincoln Kirstein speaks of being unwanted, of being 'pushed out'; Maria, in Chicago, is greatly distressed by the present standard of company performances, which, she feels, lack the true Balanchine stamp; and Brigitta, speaking of Perséphone in 1982 when Balanchine's frail life still flickered, found the company atmosphere chillingly clinical in its absorption with technique. 'I felt like an alien,' she says. Many critical views have been expressed, and there will be more, but in the end it is only the finished product, what the public sees on the stage, that is valid.

My own last sight of the City Ballet was in June 1985, at the State Theater. The programme opened with Stravinsky's *Firebird*, and for Chagall's front curtain alone I would have paid the price of my ticket. Of course I remember Fokine's ballet and saw it many times, but this didn't prevent my enjoyment of Balanchine's version. The dancing was lovely, fluid and fluent, and I was enchanted by the jewelled colours and fairytale picture-book quality of Chagall's décor and costumes. I only wished for two small changes: the Firebird herself looked a little bald and I would have given her many more fluttering feathers, and the stage lighting was too bright. The musical score has such an atmosphere of mystery that, to enhance it, I would have preferred murky gloom and vivid pools of light.

The remainder of the evening was pure dancing – marvellous Balanchine choreography, beautifully and effortlessly performed. On leaving the theatre I realized that I was smiling with pleasure and gratitude. Even if small changes of emphasis and style are creeping into the work of this great company, it is still in a category of its own, just as Bob Irving said. And I cannot believe that, based on such sound foundations, it can easily change.

And Balanchine himself – how is his reputation today, both professionally and personally? As a professional, he seems to bring out the extremes of reaction in most people – the Americans reaching a point of near-deification, and the British coming close to total dismissal. Clive Barnes though conceding Balanchine's importance to classical ballet, thinks he was 'greatly over-rated'; Edwin Denby thought him the master of masters and a genius. Lincoln Kirstein and the City Ballet, needless to say, agree, and so does Alicia Markova. But most of the British ballet world give, first, faint praise and then start to pick away at the fabric of Balanchine's work until there is precious little left. I find the American adoration overblown but understandable, particularly among those who worked with him, but I deplore – and will never understand – the British attitude. It is not only ungenerous, it is blind.

Ninette de Valois is one of the very few with something
positive and constructive to say. For many of his abstract
ballets, which she has never greatly liked, she visualizes a new
form of performance. Speaking of the intense musicality of his
work, she would like to see these abstracts danced, in practice
clothes, in a large arena like the Royal Albert Hall in London –
with the full orchestra seated round the perimeter. They would
be 'concert ballets' and usher in a new form of entertainment. I
wish such an experiment could be tried.

As a man, the public knows Balanchine through the press
and the many interviews he gave, which are filled with quot-
able sayings and with his sometimes impenetrable humour. His
single-mindedness of purpose and, I think, his self-centredness,
were always evident and, as with everyone, he said both
sensible and silly things. One of his more thoughtless was the
statement, 'I always say, just dance, don't act. Dancers who act
can't dance very well.' He cannot have seen the work of the
Canadian Lynn Seymour. Perhaps he said 'Ballet is Woman'
only once, but this is quoted so consistently that it has become a
bore and is, to me, almost incomprehensible. But he also said,
'Put sixteen girls on a stage and it's everybody – the world. Put
sixteen boys and it's nobody.' Yet, for me, the most exciting
dancing I have ever seen in my life was exclusively male – men
in uniform, the Red Army State Dancers.

But for every one of these woolly, ill thought-out phrases he
could be wonderfully perceptive and imaginative about his
work and his theatrical philosophy. He always communicated
best with his dancers, using imagery which gave them insights
into their work and which revealed much of his own personality. He also said many delightfully simple things. Disliking
programme notes, which he considered unnecessary, he said,
'The curtain should just go up and if the spectators understand
what's going on, it's good – if not, not.' To Jerome Robbins, who
was at an unsettled moment of his choreographic career, he
said, 'Just keep making ballets, and every once in a while one
will be a masterpiece.' And after reading a fulsome article, and
speaking to no one in particular, he said, 'Publicity over-rates
everything. Picasso's over-rated. I'm over-rated. Even Jack
Benny's over-rated.'

Index